MW01047190

# Basic
# Principles
## of
# New
# Age
### Thought

# Basic Principles of New Age Thought

by Dr. John Eidsmoe

New Leaf Press

**Green Forest, Arkansas**

**FIRST EDITION**
**1991**

Library of Congress Catalog Number: 91-061716

ISBN: 0-89221-208-X

## Dedication

To my wife Marlene and to our children, David, Kirsten and Justin.

# Contents

*CHAPTER ONE*

# FROM THE AGE OF SPUTNIK TO THE AGE OF AQUARIUS
## *or CARL SAGAN, MEET DARTH VADER*

"This is the dawning of the Age of Aquarius!"

Many of us remember this song from the 1960s. Perhaps we even sang it ourselves. Most of us didn't know what it meant. We thought the Age of Aquarius was just another fad or a trendy way of ushering in a new decade — and after the turbulent 60s anything would be an improvement!

Few of us realized that the Age of Aquarius was a religious concept — as religious as the Millennial Rule of Christ. The Age of Aquarius, like the Age of Pisces that preceded it, is a period of time (roughly a thousand years, to strengthen the comparison to the biblical Millennium) during which the astrological sign of Aquarius, and with it the house of Aquarius, has the ascendency in the Zodiac. This means the cosmic atmosphere of that portion of the Zodiac represented by Aquarius reigns supreme over the earth, and the house of Aquarius will have the primary influence over events on earth. The result, we are told, will be an age of greater spiritual awareness and heightened cosmic consciousness. It will be an age of renewed interest in the supernatural.

From 1967 to 1970 I was a law student at the University of Iowa. Despite Iowa's image as a conservative midwestern state, the university was a hotbed of radicalism. This was the age of student demonstrations, the Students for a Democratic Society, the drive to close down the country to stop the Vietnam war — from the standpoint of a conservative Christian activist, a dark age indeed.

Something of a hotblooded radical myself, but of the opposite kind, I recall fistfighting with SDS radicals, even risking my life to help two war veterans escape the wrath of a leftist mob. As a conservative columnist for the University of Iowa student newspaper, the *Daily Iowan* (we of the conservative underground nicknamed it the "Daily Idiot"), I loved to satirize the New Left, and during the Cambodia riots of 1970 I slept with a rifle under my bed because of threatening phone calls. It was a turbulent time, and it was also a time of transition — a transition that continues through today.

During this time I managed the Campus Crusade for Christ house in Iowa City. Many of us were immersed in battling the University's radical establishment. I know it sounds like a contradiction to speak of a "radical establishment," but radicals need establishments just like the rest of us — and their very radicalism causes them to run their political machines with greater self-righteous zeal and vengeance. And during the fall of 1967, the radical establishment that ran the University of Iowa was rocked with a seemingly new and unorthodox idea: They were hit squarely in the face with the challenging thought that Jesus Christ is relevant to the problems of today!

One afternoon every week, the student center at the University of Iowa held a "soap box soundoff," an open forum at which any budding student orator could take the microphone and speak out on the issues of the day. Normally the radical left dominated soapbox soundoff, and Vietnam occupied most of their attention. Sometimes student conservatives from the Young Americans for Freedom challenged them, but only on secular terms.

But one day, to the surprise of everyone, several clean-cut young members of Campus Crusade for Christ took the microphone. They declared that the problems of war, racism and poverty were rooted in the sinful nature of man, and that the only solution for sin was the Lord Jesus Christ and the salvation He purchased for us on the Cross.

The radicals were dumfounded! They were confronted with arguments they had not considered and could not refute. But the significance was greater than that. They didn't realize it, and neither did I, but these Marxist denizens who had ruled the murky waters of academia for decades were fast becoming ideological dinosaurs. Their Age of Humanism was drawing to a close. They were becoming extinct!

Their world was crumbling. In its place was dawning the Age of Aquarius. In the spring of 1970 one of my Campus Crusade friends spoke of the Age of Aquarius.

He saw it as a rebirth of spiritual interest in which millions of people would turn to Jesus Christ.

He was right in a sense. The Age of Aquarius is indeed bringing a rebirth of spiritual interest. But not everything spiritual is good. Satan is a spirit, and he definitely is not good. The renewed interest in the supernatural had both good and bad ramifications

Had I been more perceptive, I might have seen the negative side of the Age of Aquarius. Even in my rudimentary way, I sensed that this new spiritual interest was not entirely in accord with God's Word. The flower children of the counterculture professed a love of nature and a desire for oneness with nature that almost bespoke reverence and presaged the pantheism of the New Age movement. The fascination with Eastern mysticism, the rejection of orthodox Christianity, and the repudiation of Western rationalism which is both the nemesis of Christianity and yet also the product of Christianity, were harbingers of things to come. Even the renewed interest in Jesus was conditioned on recreating Him as a guru, a hippie, a pacifist, a revolutionary, and the ultimate drug trip rolled into one (The Jesus people! "Turn on to Jesus!" remember?). But God in His sovereign grace allowed many to go through this phase of Jesus-worship in order that He might lead them to true faith in His Son, the Second person of the Trinity, the Lord Jesus Christ.

Nevertheless, a change had taken place. No longer could secularism reign supreme in academia, in the media, and American public life. No longer would materialist assumptions go unchallenged in public debate. Secular Humanism found itself confronted by many forms of supernaturalism of both the right and the wrong kind. In short, Secular Humanism had come face to face with the Age of Aquarius.

C.S. Lewis, one of the most perceptive and insightful thinkers of our time, saw this transition coming. A British intellectual who turned to Christ, Lewis expressed orthodox concepts in original and interesting ways. Lewis wrote *The Screwtape Letters* during World War II; they were printed in book form in 1960. The premise of *The*

*Screwtape Letters* is that Satan has assigned a demon to each human being, called a "patient," to keep that person as far as possible from God (referred to as "the Enemy"). Taking the form of letters of advice from a senior demon named Screwtape to a junior demon named Wormwood to advise Wormwood how best to handle his "patient," *The Screwtape Letters* give interesting insight into Satan, demons, and the working of the human mind. In letter number seven Screwtape writes,

My Dear Wormwood,

I wonder you should ask me whether it is essential to keep the patient ignorant of your own existence. That question, at least for the present phase of the struggle, has been answered for us by the High Command (Satan). Our policy, for the moment, is to conceal ourselves. Of course this has not always been so. We are really faced with a cruel dilemma. When the humans disbelieve in our existence we lose all the pleasing results of direct terrorism, and we make no magicians. On the other hand, when they believe in us, we cannot make them materialists and skeptics. At least, not yet. I have great hopes that we shall learn in due time how to emotionalize and mythologize their science to such an extent that what is, in effect, a belief in us (though not under that name) will creep in while the human mind remains closed to belief in the Enemy [God]. The "Life Force," the worship of sex, and some aspects of psychoanalysis may here prove useful. If once we can produce our perfect work — the Materialist Magician, the man, not using, but veritably worshiping, what he vaguely calls "Forces" while denying the existence of "spirits" — then the end of the war will be in sight. But in the meantime we must obey our orders. I do not think you will have much difficulty in keeping the patient in the dark. The fact that "devils" are predominantly comic figures in the modern imagination will help you. If any faint suspicion of your existence begins to arise in his mind, suggest to him a picture of something in red tights, and persuade him that since he cannot believe in that (it is an old textbook method of confusing them) he therefore cannot believe in you.[1]

The transition C.S. Lewis foresaw is upon us today: from the Age of the Materialist to the Age of the Magician, from the Age of Humanism that reigned for several decades to the New Age that is dawning. Carl Sagan, meet Darth Vader!

The Age of Humanism could not last long. Man soon ceases to find satisfaction in self-worship, and he then moves on to something else. The first chapter of Romans details man's regression from self-worship to paganism:

> ... when they knew God, they glorified him not as God, neither were thankful; but became vain in their imaginations, and their foolish heart was darkened. Professing themselves to be wise, they became fools, And changed the glory of the incorruptible God into an image made like to corruptible man, and to birds, and four-footed beasts, and creeping things. Wherefore God also gave them up to uncleanness through the lusts of their own hearts, to dishonor their own bodies between themselves: Who changed the truth of God into a lie, and worshiped and served the creature more than the Creator, who is blessed for ever. Amen (Rom. 1:21-25).

For ultimately Humanism is an unsatisfying faith and an extremely narrow world view. It limits man's perspective to that which he can perceive with his five senses. Seeing, hearing, tasting, touching, and smelling nothing greater than himself, the Humanist worships man by making man the supreme value in the universe.

But deep inside, man knows his own inadequacy. Ultimately he seeks something besides himself to worship. He deifies natural objects, created things — rocks, trees, animals, graven images — and worships them as though they were gods. He attributes supernatural powers to them, and in his mind they come to represent powerful forces of nature. This is the essence of the old paganism. It is also the essence of the New Age, which is simply the old paganism revived.

We commonly polarize science and religion as though they were opposites, and we treat anything supernatural (whether New Age occultism or orthodox Christianity) as religion. For one who holds a strictly materialistic world view, that is a natural conclusion.

Everything that is allegedly supernatural is unreal, hallucinatory, and can be lumped together as mythology and folklore. It matters little what "myths" one chooses to believe in — the biblical prophecy of the second coming of Christ and His victory over Satan and the armies of the earth or the Norse myth of the final battle of the gods and the frost giants, Armageddon or Ragnarok, Heaven or Valhalla.

The prayers of a saint and the incantations of a witch are all one and the same. In opposition to both stand the findings of the scientist, the voice of reason and reality.

But religion and magic are not the same, and science is not their opposite. As Jeffrey Burton Russell has observed in *Witchcraft In the Middle Ages*, there is "an essential link between science and magic much stronger than that between religion and magic."[2] Russell notes that during the Middle Ages and the Renaissance the Church "made every effort to restrain magic, high and low, whereas natural scientists eagerly pursued magical practices."[3] Consider the medieval sorcerer and his magic caldron, as he eagerly pursued alchemy (the belief that matter could be changed from one element to another, such as iron to gold — a view that made good sense in the pagan and New Age view of reality) as the highest science of his day.

Not only were the leading scientists of the Renaissance magicians, Russell says,

> ...the very nature of their scientific work and their attitudes were magical. The opposition of the Church to some of the developments of natural science in the Renaissance was consequently part and parcel of its resistance to magic. In these sorcerer-scientists Christianity was opposing the magical world view that it

had opposed since the days of Simon Magus; science had not yet developed its own world view and to a great extent accepted that of magic.⁴

The essential link between magic and science — modern materialistic science, that is, not the true science that humbly seeks to understand and apply the physical laws established by the Creator — lies in the basic definition of magic, which sets forth its basic difference with religion. As Russell says, "magic attempts to compel the powers of the Universe; religion supplicates them."⁵ As the Swedish theologian Nathan Soderblom says, "The essence of religion is submission and trust. The essence of magic is audacious self-glorification. Magic knows no bounds to its power; religion, in the proper sense, begins when man feels his impotence in the face of a power which fills him with awe and dread. ... Magic is thus in direct opposition to the spirit of religion."⁶

The difference is this: True religion, specifically Christianity, prostrates itself before the throne of God, acknowledges man's inadequacy and helplessness before Him, and implores His gracious help. Magic, on the other hand, seeks to control the forces of the universe, be they natural forces or supernatural. (The reader is urged to consider to what extent some elements of modern Christianity, particularly "prosperity" teaching, have crossed the line from religion into magic. Instead of seeking the grace of a sovereign God, they see Him as a genie in a bottle who can be controlled and manipulated into doing the will of man if we just learn to rub the bottle with the right words and prayers.) Like magic, science seeks to enable man to control the forces of nature. In this way science and magic are similar, while religion is their opposite.

There are some differences. Magic accepts supernatural reality; science does not — not that all scientists necessarily reject all belief in the supernatural, but the modern scientific method allows no room for its consideration. The magician and the scientist both seek to control the universe. But the magician's world view is broader than the scientist's; the magical world view allows for more than the five senses can apprehend. Likewise the magician's solutions are less precise. The scientist deals with physical reality and discovers and formulates precise scientific laws to explain them. The magician deals with physical reality and nonphysical reality as well. His world view includes a realm in which the physical laws of cause and effect do not necessarily apply; consequently his remedies and laws are broader but also less precise.

Despite their similarity, antagonism exists between some modern scientists and the occult. As Dr. Gary North observes in his excellent book *Unholy Spirits,* "Modern science cannot handle the facts of paranormal science."[7] Confronted with evidence of supernatural healing, whether Christian or occult, modern science is forced to deny that such phenomena occur, or offer the most far-fetched naturalistic explanations, or impugn the integrity of those who offer such evidence, or if all else fails, simply ignore the evidence. "Isn't it far better to admit that a peasant can fool you than to admit that a peasant can have access to powers that dwarf anything a trained physician can do?"[8]

The same is true of UFOs. "The critics respond by trotting out every disproved sighting and representative crackpot encounters, but they studiously, scientifically avoid the hard cases where the evidence of simultaneous sightings by hundreds of people can be proven to have taken place. The skeptics perceive that if such events are true, then modern science isn't. They would then have to revise the presuppositions of modern autonomous science in order to make it into something quite foreign, something dangerously close to the cosmic personalism of the Bible, or the cosmic personalism of primitive animist religion."[9]

The result is that UFOs are either denied or explained as natural phenomena:

> People who have no particular theological beliefs, people who do not espouse the doctrines of New Age humanism, or ancient mysticism, nevertheless can be persuaded that there are such phenomena as flying saucers. They are seen as phenomena [physical real-

ity], not noumena [supernatural reality]. They can be explained as technological wonders from beings who have advanced technology beyond mankind.

The basis of this faith in the technological reality of flying saucers is that there can be other beings outside of this world who are nevertheless limited by the natural laws and scientific laws of this world. It is assumed, in other words, that creatures beyond earth's atmosphere here have somehow gained access to certain kinds of knowledge that enable them to visit the earth. This sort of knowledge, however, is knowledge which in principle can be understood by scientific man. They are better scientists than we are, but they are not occult magicians. They are better builders than we are today, but given enough money and enough formulas and enough skills, General Motors in principle will be able to produce interstellar or intergalactic or at least interplanetary spaceships.[10]

The problem is, the evidence indicates that UFOs are not simply visitors from another planet. There is no consistency to UFO design, and the UFOs do not seem to adhere to physical laws of cause and effect: They can travel at fantastic speed and come to an instant and complete stop; their travel at enormous speeds do not seem to produce heat; they abruptly change direction and sometimes suddenly change shape or disappear. Dr. North suggests that UFOs are really a demonic manifestation, and that is a possibility scientists must reject at all costs:

> Scientists may worry about the Bomb, or the potential plague threat of a newly created test tube bacteria, but the idea that there are forces in this world that in

principle cannot be explained by repeatable cause-and-effect laws scares them even more. They are men clinging to a dying paradigm — a paradigm that was never fully accepted by residents in the West, and which was never accepted at all by residents in primitive cultures. They are fighting for survival, not just as guild members who are about to be replaced, but as members of a guild which as a whole cannot survive if an invasion from the pnoumenal [spirit world] is taken seriously.

If the saucers are in fact operated by little green men from the stars, scientists will find a way to cope with the problem. But conventional scientists smell trouble. The evidence points to something other than men from Mars. Men from Mars are in principle no different from amoebas from Mars, and scientists have been almost religious in their pursuit of evidence of life forms on the planets (as evidence of Darwinian evolution). No, what bothers them is that the stories associated with UFO phenomena indicate that we are dealing with noumena: invasions from a world beyond mathematical cause and effect. Such forces do not belong here. They point to even greater forces, the traditional forces of heaven and hell, of final judgment. These are far more serious than invaders from Mars.[11]

The heart of the matter, then, is that many modern scientists act and think and draw conclusions, not strictly according to rules of evidence, but to sustain and further their basic faith in their rationalistic and materialistic world view:

"The typical Western rationalist, being a materialist, cannot accept the possibility that there are forces that can affect the visible, measurable world that do not conform to the laws of the world — laws that are at bottom the laws of the self-proclaimed autonomous reason of man."[12]

Modern scientists, to maintain their world view, must reject such phenomena as UFOs, supernatural healing, astral projection, ESP, divination of the future, psychics who can solve crimes or find missing persons and the like. Such possibilities, Dr. North says, represent "a reenchantment of the world."[13] A resurrection of the world of the magician. The dawning of the Age of Aquarius.

The New Age.

But despite these differences, and in spite of the dilemma in which Western rationalism finds itself, the essential link remains: Modern science and ancient magic, the materialist and the magician, both seek to control the forces of the universe. And for this reason both are the antithesis of true religion.

And in this way modern science and ancient magic are both humanistic, for both seek the glorification of man. As Russell says,

> The essence of the magical world view is belief in a homocentric [man-centered] universe. Man is literally the microcosm reflecting the macrocosm, so that the macrocosm in turn is a projection of man. Hence all things — stars, herbs, stones, metals, planets, the elements, and elementals — mesh with man, his longings, his lusts, his desires, his fears, and even his physical apearance and health. Each natural object and natural phenomenon has a direct influence upon some aspect of man's body or psyche, and man's actions

can in turn affect the elements. All things are made for man and on the model of man. Magic is a doctrine that, far more than religion or science, exalts man to the loftiest regions of glory: hence its perennial attraction, and hence its particular appeal for the Renaissance, when man's ambitions and his ability to achieve them seemed unlimited.[14]

The microcosm in the macrocosm! What the universe does controls the destiny of man, and at the same time what man does controls the forces of the universe. As the old occult saying goes, "As above, so below."[15] Magic is man's attempt to control and manipulate these forces. Some have distinguished between "high magic" and "low magic:"

Low and high magic, although they sometimes meet, have always been different. In the Middle Ages, for example, theologians like Alexander of Hales distinguished clearly between divination, the central aspect of high magic, and maleficium, evil-doing, the central aspect of low magic. Low magic is practical and aimed at obtaining immediate effects, for example, urinating into a ditch to cause rain or sticking a wax doll with a pin to cause pain; high magic is akin to religious, scientific, and philosophical speculation and reaches out through occult knowledge to understand, grasp, and ultimately control the Universe.[16]

By this time it should be aparent that in studying the New Age and the occult we are not looking at something simple. Nor are we talking about games or child's play. Pagans are not stupid or simplistic or irreligious; theirs is a highly complex religion and a comprehensive world view. But it is a religion and world view which is diametrically at odds with Christianity. As Russell begins his book,

> To understand witchcraft we must descend into the darkness of the deepest oceans of the mind. In our efforts to avoid facing the realities of human evil, we have tamed the witch and made her comic, dressing her in a peaked cap and setting her on a broom for the amusement of children at Halloween. Thus made silly she can easily be exorcised from our minds, and we convince our children — and ourselves — that "there is no such thing as a witch." But there is, or at least there was. A phenomenon that for centuries gripped the minds of men from the most illiterate peasant to the most skilled philosopher or scientist, leading to torture and death for hundreds of thousands, is neither joke nor illusion.[17]

The New Age movement, for all its attractions and for all its claims to gentleness, is essentially a power religion — the antithesis of true religion. That being the case, can the New Age movement be called a religion at all?

The Founders of this nation would not have thought so. In enacting the First Amendment they certain had no intention of protecting anything related to the occult.

But recent Supreme Court decisions have defined religion more broadly. For example, in *Thomas* vs. *Review Board*, 450 U.S. 707 (1981), the Court said a viewpoint is considered religious if it is based upon religious training and belief, regardless of whether it is specifically embodied in the official creed of a church. In *U. S.* vs. *Seeger*, 380 U.S. 163 (1965), the Court held that for purposes of the Selective Service laws, a religious belief did not even have to embody faith in a transcendent God, or any god at all; if the belief is sincere and deeply held and involves ultimate concern with whatever occupies in the adherent's mind the place God normally holds in the mind of the orthodox believer, the viewpoint will be considered religious.

And in *Torcaso* vs. *Watkins*, 367 U.S. 488 (1961), the Court even recognized Secular Humanism as a religion:

> 11. Among religions in this country which do not teach what would generally be considered a belief in the existence of God are Buddhism, Taoism, Ethical Culture, Secular Humanism, and others....

Since the New Age movement recognizes a spiritual reality, offers explanations for man's origin, man's place in the present universe, and man's ultimate destiny, and offers diagnoses and solutions for man's basic spiritual problems, the New Age movement must be considered a religion. For this reason, to the same extent the establishment clause of the First Amendment prohibits public schools and other public entities from promoting the doctrines and practices of Christianity, to the same extent the First Amendment also prohibits the establishment of the New Age movement through public school curricula and other means.

But what, really, is the New Age movement? Many authors have gone to great lengths to document the New Age connections of various persons — how so-and-so belongs to such-and-such organization which has an interlocking directorate with another organization which publicly espouses New Age beliefs, and so forth. It is important to know about these connections.

But few writers really tell us what the New Age movement is all about. We can characterize the New Age as globalism, feminism, and the like, and it is true that most New Agers believe in these causes. But that doesn't really tell us what the New Age movement is.

What do New Agers believe? What are their underlying presuppositions? What is their basic world view? And how does the New Age movement affect you, your children, your school, your church, your work place, your community, and your nation?

This book provides some answers to these questions. In this book, I present a systematic analysis of New Age thought, devoting a chapter to each of the basic remises of New Age philosophy and contrasting these with biblical Christianity: (1) Rejection of Absolute Reality; (2) Impersonalism of God and man; (3) Nature is God; (4) Evolution;

(5) Man is God; (6) We create our own reality; and (7) The need to achieve conscious union with the god of nature.

The book closes with practical advice on how to recognize, resist and confront the New Age.

So — have you ever been caught up short when someone stopped you in mid-sentence and asked, "New Age? What's that?" have you fumbled for words, uttering half-coherent phrases about humanism, globalism, feminism, Satanism, and the like, knowing in your own mind that these are aspects of the New Age movement, but also knowing that you haven't really explained what the New Age is and how these various aspects relate to the New Age movement and to each other?

After reading this book, you will be able to explain these matters — to yourself and to others. And understanding the New Age, you will be better equipped to combat it.

But first, a word of caution. As C.S. Lewis observes in his preface to *The Screwtape Letters*, there are two dangers in dealing with devils: ignorance, and an unhealthy interest[18]. If we are ignorant of Satan and his demonic allies, we are vulnerable to their deception. But like the vice squad officer who becomes so wrapped up in investigating and prosecuting vice that he falls into sin himself, it is possible to become so immersed in studying and combatting the New Age movement that we become captured by it — and there is much about the New Age that fascinates, attracts, and captivates. Before undertaking any study of the New Age, it is vitally important to be under the authority of a church, in close fellowship with other Christian believers, and in close communication with the Triune God through prayer and the regular study of His Word, the Bible.

We therefore urge you, every time you pick up this book, to preface your reading of it with a prayer that God will preserve you from both of these dangers.

Ready? Then come with us as we eagerly, but prayerfully and carefully, examine the mysteries of the New Age movement.

## ENDNOTES

1. C.S. Lewis, *The Screwtape Letters* (New York: Macmillan, 1961, 1968), pp. 32-33.

2. Jeffrey Burton Russell, *Witchcraft In The Middle Ages* (Ithaca, New York: Cornell University Press, 1972), p. 11.

3. Ibid.

4. Ibid., pp. 11-12.

5. Ibid. p. 10, citing Sir James Frazier, *The Golden Bough* (London, 1911), I:xx.

6. Nathan Soderblom, *The Living God* (London, 1933), p. 36; quoted by Russell, Ibid., p. 10.

7. Gary North, *Unholy Spirits: Occultism and*

*New Age Humanism* (Ft. Worth: Dominion Press, 1986), p. 238.

   8. Ibid., P. 263.

   9. Ibid., pp. 302-303.

   10. Ibid., P. 304.

   11. Ibid. p. 314.

   12. Ibid., p.321.

   14. Russell, op. cit., p. 5.

   15. Colin Wilson, *The Occult: A History* (New York, Random House, 1971), pp. 193, 232

   16. Russell, op. cit., pp. 6-7

   17. Ibid., p. 1.

   18. Lewis, op. cit., p. 3

*CHAPTER TWO*

# REJECTION OF ABSOLUTE REALITY

For over a thousand years, tales of the Knights of the Round Table have inspired the Western world. As a child I read of Arthur the wise king, Gwenevere his fair queen, Lancelot the brave and valiant knight, Galahad the purehearted knight who achieved the quest for the Holy Grail, Mordred the villainous traitor, Merlin the benevolent scientist/magician, and Morgana the evil queen who dabbled in the black arts. To what extent the King Arthur legends are rooted in historical reality, no one knows for sure. But these stories of imperfect men and women who strove after Christian ideals have been treasured for countless generations.

But times are changing, and the King Arthur legends have been rewritten for the Age of Aquarius. Marion Zimmer Bradley, in her widely-selling novel *The Mists of Avalon*, tells the legend of Camelot through the eyes of Morgana (or Morgaine, as she is called in the novel, using the old Celtic forms). The scene is Britain around the fifth century, and as Rome has retreated and left the Britons to themselves, Christianity and paganism are battling for the soul of the nation. But in Bradley's novel the pagans are the "good guys," and Morgana is cast as the heroine. As a pagan priestess she is intelligent, strong-willed, mostly benevolent, clear of purpose, and sort of a fifth-century feminist.

By contrast Gwenevere (Gwynyfar) is a fanatical Christian and a sniveling and confused weakling who despite her professed Christian morality still succumbs to her desire for Lancelot. Arthur and Lancelot are torn between the two faiths, professing Christianity largely for political reasons but inwardly longing for the old pagan ways. Merlin is the wise pagan priest and seer who, in the magnanimous style of an open-minded professor, sees value and truth in all religions, including Christianity. It is an entertaining and engrossing novel, but also it is skillful propaganda for the New Age.

Avalon in legend is an island in the western sea, sometimes identified with America and sometimes as a pagan version of Heaven or Valhalla. It is also a name for Glastonbury, a misty island in a swampy inlet drained by the River Brue in southwest England. Glastonbury has a rich history for Christians and Pagans alike, being an ancient center for Druid worship and also the site of a very old Christian church and monastery.

According to tradition, Joseph of Arimethea brought the Gospel to Britain and made Glastonbury his home[1].

In *The Mists of Avalon*, Avalon and Glastonbury are two dimensions of reality, a place where the walls between the Christian world and the Pagan world are thin and where it is easy to pass from one to the other. On this island, in one dimension of reality, the Pagan Priestess, the Lady of the Lake, trains her novices and performs her rites for the Mother Goddess, while in the other dimension the Christian monks of Glastonbury offer their hymns and prayers to Jesus Christ. As Morgana says,

> There was a time when a traveller, if he had the will and knew only a few of the secrets, could send his barge out into the Summer Sea and arrive not at Glastonbury of the monks, but at the Holy Isle of Avalon; for at that time the gates of the worlds drifted within the mists, and were open, one to another, as the traveller thought and willed. For this is the great secret, which was known to all educated men in our day: that by what men think, we create the world around us, daily new.
>
> And now the priests, thinking that this infringes upon the power of their God, who created the world once and for all to be unchanging, have closed those doors (which were never doors, except in the minds of men), and the pathway leads only to the priests' Isle, which they have safeguarded with the sound of their church bells, driving away all thoughts of another world lying in the darkness. Indeed, they say that world, if it indeed exists, is the property of Satan, and the doorway to Hell, if not Hell itself.[2]

In the prologue to the story, Morgana speaks, setting forth her pagan world view:

> For this is the thing the priests do not know, with their One God and One Truth: that there is no such thing as a true tale. Truth has many faces and the truth is like to the old road to Avalon; it depends on your own will, and your own thoughts, whither the road will take you, and whether, at the end, you arrive in the Holy Isle of Eternity or among the priests with their bells and their death and their Satan and Hell and damnation ... but perhaps I am unjust even to them. Even the Lady of the Lake, who hated a priest's robe as she would have hated a poisonous viper, and with good cause too, chid me once for speaking evil of their God.
>
> "For all the Gods are one God," she said to me then, as she had said many times before, and as I have said to my own novices many times, and as every priestess who comes after me will say again, "and all the Goddesses are one Goddess, and their is only one Initiator. And to every man his own truth, and the God within."[3]

Morgana and Arthur, as half-siblings, have a tempestuous relationship, for King Arthur has embraced Christianity. For the world is becoming Christian, and the days of wizards are fading. But Arthur still longs for the Pagan paths, and in the end Paganism claims him:

> ...I could greet Arthur at last, when he lay dying, not as my enemy and the enemy of my Goddess, but only as my brother, and as a dying man in need of the Mother's aid, where all men come at last. Even the priests know this, with their ever-virgin Mary in her blue robe; for she too becomes the World Mother in the

hour of death.

And so Arthur lay at last with his head in my lap, seeing in me neither sister nor lover nor foe, but only wise-woman, priestess, Lady of the Lake; and so rested upon the breast of the Great Mother from whom he came to birth and to whom at last, as all men, he must go. And perhaps, as I guided the barge which bore him away, not this time to the Isle of the Priests, but to the true Holy Isle in the dark world behind our own, that Island of Avalon where, now, few but I could go, he repented the emnity that had come between us.[4]

As Morgana's words fall upon twentieth century readers who are conditioned to prize open-mindedness above all other values, paganism claims the high ground. Pagans are broad-minded enough to tolerate Christianity, but Christians are too narrow-minded to tolerate paganism. The pagan priests could accept the "White Christ" as another god, perhaps even worship Him. But Christians insist that their God is the only God, and all others are either demons or nonexistent. Unlike the benevolent, tolerant pagan gods, the Christian God is a jealous tyrant who demands our exclusive allegiance. Morgana is thus justified in resenting the Christian God; but perhaps the fault really lies not with the Christian God but rather with Christians — "the monks at Glastonbury" — who have misrepresented their God.

*The Mists of Avalon* is not alone in glorifying Morgana. Joan Wolf, in her novel *The Road To*

*Avalon* (New York: Penguin Books, 1988), treats Morgana (Morgan, in her book) as the heroine of Camelot and King Arthur's one true love.

These are in marked contrast to the earlier versions of the King Arthur stories, which portray the knights of the Round Table as Christian gentlemen dedicated to the service of God and the medieval code of chivalry. Read, for example, some of the earlier works like Sir Thomas Mallory's fifteenth century work *Le Morte D'Arthur: The Book of King Arthur and His Knights of the Round Table* (New Hyde Park, New York: University Books, 1961). For a modern, abridged version of Mallory's works, try *King Arthur and His Knights: Selected Tales By Sir Thomas Mallory*, ed. Eugene Vinaver (New York: Oxford, 1975); or John Steinbeck's *The Acts of King Arthur and His Noble Knights* (New York: Ballentine, 1976). Other portrayals depict King Arthur as his knights as virtuous, chivalrous, Christian men: Alfred, Lord Tennyson's *Idylls Of The King*; Edmund Spenser's *Fairie Queene*; the fourteenth century English poem *Sir Gawain and the Green Knight*; the thirteenth century Grail romances such as *Parzival* and *Queste Adel Saint Graal*; the twelfth century *Tristan Und Isolde* or the *Mabinogion*, a collection of old Welsh tales.

Twentieth century retellings of the King Arthur tales continue the Christian world view: Howard Pyle's *The Story Of King Arthur and His Knights*

(New York: Dover, 1903 1965) and *The Story of the Champions of the Round Table* (New York: Dover, 1905, 1968); T.H. White's *The Once and Future King* (New York: Berkley Medallion, 1939, 1966); or my own childhood favorite from which I derived much Christian inspiration, *King Arthur For Boys* by Henry Gilbert (Chicago: Saalfield, n.d.) A fascinating modern rendition by Stephen R. Lawhead depicts Arthur as a devoted Christian king who triumphs over the forces of Paganism. Called *The Pendragron Cycle*, it consists of three volumes: *Taliesin, Merlin,* and *Arthur* (Westchester, Illinois: Crossway, 1988, 1989).

Or to see this contrast in living color, go to your video store and order the 1956 MGM movie, *Knights of the Round Table,* and the 1984 Warner Bros. *Excalibur.* The former depicts chivalrous, virtuous knights who hold a clear Christian world view, whereas the latter is steeped in the occult, in hedonism, immorality and gory violence. In *Excalibur* even the Holy Grail becomes an occult symbol from which the King of England derives power.

The actual events of those times, as well as the origins of the King Arthur legends, are shrouded in mystery; and there are Christian and pagan themes intertwined. I mention these to illustrate the way modern writers and producers have incorporated pagan themes to advance the New Age.

Morgana's words in *The Mists of Avalon* — "to every man his own truth, and the God within" — well summarize the first premise of New Age thought: rejection of absolute reality. Or, as some put it, perception is reality. Truth is whatever you perceive it to be.

For the traditional Western mind, this is difficult to grasp. Westerners commonly think of reality as objective and absolute. Reality isn't created in your mind; it's "out there." The process of truth-seeking is finding out what really is "out there" and adjusting our thinking accordingly. Some Western thinkers like Descartes and Kant have argued that our perceptions may be far different from the way things really are, but they do not deny that objective reality exists.

For example, as you read this book, you may feel the urge to stretch your legs out on a footstool. Now, either that footstool is there, or it isn't. You can't conjure up that footstool in your mind, and then rest your feet on it! And in the Western view, truth is objective. An idea is true or false, or it may contain some elements of truth and some elements of falsity. But our perception does not affect the idea. If the idea is true, and I do not believe in it, then I am wrong! If the idea is false, my belief in it does not make it true. Rather, my belief is wrong!

Also central to the Western idea of truth is the law of noncontradiction. Truth cannot contradict other truth. If two ideas contradict each other, then one or the other (or both) is wrong.

The story is told of the blind men who came in contact with an elephant. One, feeling the elephant's tail, said "This animal is long and thin like a rope." Another, feeling his tusk, said "This animal is hard as a rock." Another, feeling his belly, said "This animal is large and heavy." The fourth, feeling his leg, said, "This animal is like a post."

Each of their observations was accurate as far as it went. And they weren't contradicting each other. Each had only an incomplete portion of the whole animal.

In the same way truth can have many facets, but truth cannot contradict other truth. If A is true, then any idea that contradicts A must be false. Each of us may have a different part of the truth, but those parts cannot contradict each other.

Suppose Jesus had said, "You can come to the Father through me." Suppose, further, that someone today says, "I can come to the Father through Buddha or Mohammed." There's no logical contradiction here. Given this information alone, it is possible that there could be more than one way of coming to the Father.

But that's not what Jesus said. He said, "I am the way, the truth, and the life: no man cometh unto the Father, but by me" (John 14:6). By Western logic, that statement excludes all other possible ways to the Father. If Jesus was right, then anyone who says he can come to the Father through Buddha or Mohammed is wrong!

In this way the New Age movement departs from Western thought and embraces the thinking of the East. There is no objective reality; truth is whatever you perceive it to be. For perception is reality.

The New Age movement thus differs from classical Secular Humanism. The Secular Humanist has a very narrow view of reality, limiting reality to the material world that can be apprehended by the five senses. But in general he believes in objective reality, and as a Western rationalist he follows the logical law of noncontradiction. A true Secular Humanist cannot in total integrity claim to be a Christian, or a Mohammedan, or a Jew, or even a Unitarian, though there are some who call themselves religious humanists who believe that God exists but that the main purpose of religion is to serve human needs. But for the true Secular Humanist, professing faith in God would be dishonest, because he does not believe God is objectively real.

The New Ager is not bothered by this problem. Truth is as he perceives it, or as he creates it in his own mind. To every man his own truth, the New Ager says, for all paths ultimately lead to God — even Christianity. So the New Ager can fit into just about any religious system, so long as he can redefine its terminology. About the only religion he has trouble with, besides Orthodox Judaism, is conservative Christianity with its insistence upon absolute, objective truth and its assertion that Jesus Christ is the essential and only way of salvation.

In this way the New Age movement is more attractive and more dangerous than Secular Humanism. With their subjective view of reality, New Agers can fit into the church in a way that Secular Humanists could not. Many of them find various aspects of Christianity with which they can identify — Christian love, corporate unity as we are all one body in Christ, and the indwelling of the Holy Spirit in the believer, to name but a few — and so they latch onto Christianity as their personal path to God. In the process, they hope to help Christians get over some of their narrow doctrines; but rather than openly disagree with those doctrines, they redefine them for themselves in a way that is consistent with New Age thought.

Recently I had the privilege of speaking in a Catholic Church in North Dakota. Part of my theme was that the theory of evolution is more than a scientific model of origins; it is a comprehensive philosophy and world view which affects every area of human thought, and that evolutionary thought has undermined the biblical absolutes upon which Western law and our constitutional system of government are based.

Afterward a lady approached me to express her disagreement. She was a Christian, she insisted, and also a creationist. But my static view of creation was much less attractive than her dynamic view.

You see, she continued, God is energy (she expressed this as a statement of fact with which no one would disagree), and as such He must be constantly active in creation. He couldn't be content with just creating a universe in six days; rather, He began His creative work billions of years ago and continues to reform and improve His creation every day. Now, isn't this dynamic view of creation much more exciting and satisfying than my old-fashioned static view?

I had to tell her that I just couldn't accept her basic premise. Where did she get the idea that God is energy? Scripture doesn't say that! God is the source of energy; He created energy; and He possesses energy; but God Himself is not simply energy. I don't worship Energy, do you? And I am not necessarily more filled with the Spirit on days when I feel energetic, than on days when I do not. But here is a New Age concept, that of Cosmic Energy, that has been brought into the Church as a Christian point of view.

And Scripture nowhere says God is continuing to create the universe through an evolutionary process. Everything in the Bible from Genesis to

Revelation indicates that God finished His creation in six days, and then He rested: "Thus the heavens and the earth were finished, and all the host of them. And on the seventh day God ended his work which he had made; and he rested on the seventh day from all his work which he had made" (Gen. 2:1-2). God continues to interact with His creation, but the creation itself is complete.

Who is this woman? What is her goal? Is she a conscious, dedicated New Ager who is deliberately trying to deceive the Church? Possibly, but I doubt it. Most likely she sincerely believes herself to be a Christian, and she sincerely wants to improve the Church with these new, revitalized understandings that she has discovered. But they are not Christian doctrines at all; they come straight out of the New Age, disguised in Christian terminology. Possibly this woman is deliberately deceiving others; more likely she herself is deceived. In either event, she is wrong — and dangerous!

A few years ago a group of young, liberal-minded lawyers formed a legal foundation called the Christic Institute, the main goal of which seems to be the advocacy of liberal causes. Many have wondered where these lawyers derived the name for this foundation. Is "Christic" simply a trendy way of saying Christ? A leader of the Christic Institute explains that the term comes from a liberal Roman Catholic theologian and paleontologist named Pierre Teilhard de Chardin[5]. De Chardin taught that "Evolution is a general condition to which all theories, all hypotheses, all systems must bow and which they must satisfy if they are to be thinkable and true."[6] He believed there is a basic, impersonal force at work in the universe, the force that holds the universe together and keeps things moving on an even keel. De Chardin called this the "Christic force," or the "Christic principle." About two thousand years ago a young man from Nazareth named Jesus became so embued with this Christic force that he developed a oneness with it; henceforth he became known as Jesus Christ[7]. Again we have a New Age concept of God introduced into the Church as though it were a Christian principle!

Recently, while speaking in Missouri, I attended a mainline denominational church with a friend. I appreciated much of the service, but the sermon utterly amazed me.

I was aware that New Agers do not lack creativity; but how could any pastor devise a New Age sermon out of the parable of the Good Samaritan and the words of the lawyer, "And who is my neighbor?" (Luke 10:25-37).

The pastor reminded his audience that that very week was the twentieth anniversary of the first manned spacecraft landing on the moon. Because of this, he said, we must come to grips with the possibility that there may be intelligent life in other parts of the galaxy. We must therefore constantly expand our concept of "who is my neighbor?". We can no longer be content with seeing our neighbor as someone in our own community, or state, or nation. Rather, we must develop a true global consciousness, and perhaps go even beyond that to galacticism or whatever. Thus globalism, a common theme of the New Age, is introduced to a devout congregation as though it were a legitimate application of the parable taught by Jesus Christ!

Some might object that these are illegitimate applications of Scripture, for they clearly are not what Jesus meant. But the New Age movement is not concerned with such details, because the New Age has an entirely different view of reality. Margot Adler, a reporter for National Public Radio and an authority sympathetic to the New Age, explains that polytheism (belief in many gods) is a basic belief of modern neo-pagans of the New Age movement. She writes,

> The idea of polytheism is grounded in the view that reality (divine or otherwise) is multiple and diverse. And if one is a pantheist-polytheist, as are many Neo-Pagans, one might say that all nature is divinity and manifests itself in myriad forms and delightful complexities On a broader level, Isaac Bonewits wrote, "Polytheists ... develop logical systems based on multiple levels of reality and the magical Law of Infinite Universes: 'every sentient being lives in a unique universe.'"[8]

Adler also quotes Bonewits as telling her,

> The pagans were tolerant for the simple reason that
> many believed their gods and goddess to be connected
> with the people or the place. If you go to another place,
> there are different gods and goddesses, and if you're
> staying in someone else's house, you're polite to their
> gods; they're just as real as the ones you left back
> home.[9]

This is not the biblical view of truth. The Hebrew word for truth, "emeth," has its roots in that which is stable, that which is steadfast, that which has stood the test of time. There is no changing view of truth, no multiple levels of reality, no magical law of infinite universes in the Word of God.

Jesus said, "I am the way, the truth, and the life." And then He went on to make His claim exclusive: "No man cometh unto the Father, but by me" (John 14:6). In Hebrews 13:8 we read, "Jesus Christ, the same yesterday, and today, and forever." Now, if Jesus is the truth, and if Jesus doesn't change, then it follows that truth doesn't change!

Gary North describes this New Age view of reality as "Escape from Creaturehood." Refusing to accept the cosmos as it is, and refusing to accept his own limitations as a creature, the New Ager seeks to escape from reality by creating his own reality — whether through alchemy, or Transcendental Meditation, or altered states of consciousness, or alcohol or other mind-distorting drugs. But when we try to escape from reality and enter our own private world of the mind where we create our own reality, we actually cease to really work for improvement in the world around us.[10]

Paul says, "Let God be true, but every man a liar" (Rom. 3:4). "If we believe not, yet he abideth faithful: he cannot deny himself" (2 Tim 2:13).

Our Lord Jesus Christ is objective reality! If we believe in Him, He is real. But if we do not believe in Him, He remains just as real as if we do. And we will all see Him one day and bow the knee before Him. The only question is whether we behold Him as our Savior or as our Judge.

When measured against the eternal and unchanging standard of God's Word, the New Age view of truth and reality must be judged for what it really is: utterly false.

### ENDNOTES

1. E. Raymond Capt, *The Traditions of Glastonbury* (Thousand Oaks, California: Artisan Sales, 1987; William Steuart McBirnie, *The Search For The Twelve Apostles* (Wheaton, Illinois: Tyndale, 1973, 1978), pp. 211-213, 230, 289.

2. Marion Zimmer Bradley, *The Mists of Avalon* (New York: Alfred A. Knopf, 1983), p. ix.

3. Ibid., pp. x-xi.

4. Ibid., p. x.

5. Danny Sheehan, *The Constitution on Trial*,

Lecture, Boulder High School Auditorium, Boulder, Colorado, March 30, 1989, Cassette.

6. Pierre Teilhard de Chardin, quoted in *World Book Encyclopedia*, 1985, Vol. 19, "Teilhard de Chardin."

7. Sheehan, Ibid.

8. Isaac Bonewits, "The Second Epistle of Isaac," *The Druid Chronicles (Evolve)* (Berkeley: Berkeley Drunemeton Press, 1976), 2:13; quoted by Margot Adler, *Drawing Down the Moon* (Boston: Beacon Press, 1979, 1986), p. 25.

9. Bonewits, conversation with Adler, quoted by Adler, Ibid., p. 35.

10. Gary North, *Unholy Spirits: Occultism and New Age Humanism* (Fort Worth: Dominion Press, 1986), pp. 329-377.

## CHAPTER THREE

# IMPERSONALISM: GOD AND MAN

What contemporary theologian has influenced people's ideas about God more than any other?

As I travel the nation speaking about the New Age, I have asked this question of dozens of audiences. I receive many good answers: Billy Graham, Jerry Falwell, Pat Robertson, Norman Vincent Peale, Robert Schuler, many others.

Then I point out that everybody is a theologian. Most people never go to seminary, and some are less systematic in their thinking than others. But everyone has some basic ideas about God (even if it's atheism), about man, about the universe, and about the relationship between God, man and the universe.

Then I give my own nomination: George Lucas!

George Lucas, of course, is the producer of the *StarWars* trilogy. His movies — *StarWars, The Empire Strikes Back*, and *Return of the Jedi* — have reached millions of people who never darken the door of a church. And the *StarWars* trilogy does more than just make millions of dollars for Mr. Lucas. It portrays a distinctively New Age view of God, man and the universe.

What is the *StarWars* view of God? "May the Force be with you!" God is not a Person, as Christians and Jews believe, with intellect, emotion and will; He (or It) is an impersonal "Force."

Obi-Wan Kenobi, the seasoned Jedi warrior of *StarWars,* has a highly developed consciousness and is very much in touch with the Force. When Darth Vader, the villain of the story, and his allies blow up the planet "Alderaan" (the name of a demon in pagan mythology), Obi-Wan Kenobi, though millions of miles away, shudders and turns pale. When Luke Skywalker, the young Jedi warrior, asks what is wrong, Obi-Wan answers, "I felt a sudden ebbing of the Force, as if a great source of energy had come to an end. I'm not sure what it was, exactly." As Obi-Wan trains Luke to use the special laser sword called a light saber, he admonishes, "No, Luke, not so choppy. Try to feel the Force. It will direct you."

Luke asks, "Is the Force an energy field?"

Obi-Wan gives the typical answer of an Eastern mystic, "Yes, and something more. It is a nothingness that can work miracles. Once you feel it the way the Jedi knights did, you won't need an explanation." And a little later he says, "Try again, Luke. Relax. Let your mind drift. Stop thinking. Let the Force lead you."

Later Obi-Wan Kenobi is killed by Darth Vader, but his spirit lives on. And as *Star Wars* draws to a close and Luke is piloting a space fighter in an attack on the Imperial Death Star, he hears Obi-Wan's voice inside his head: "Trust me, Luke." He lets his feelings take over, fires the torpedoes, and blows up the Death Star.[1]

In the second film of the trilogy, *The Empire Strikes Back*, Luke lands on a a gloomy, cloud-covered planet called Dagobah. There he meets a little creature called Yoda, the archetype of an Eastern guru. Yoda instructs Luke further about the Force:

> ... my ally is the Force. A powerful ally it is. Life creates it and makes it grow. Its energy surrounds us. Feel it you must. Feel the flow. Feel the Force around you. Here between us and there between that tree and that rock. Everywhere, waiting to be used.[2]

This is more than entertainment and fiction, for entertaining fiction is a valuable way to implant ideas. When you read an editorial in the newspaper, your guard is up; you evaluate critically as you read, asking yourself whether you agree or disagree. But when you read the comic section or watch a movie, your guard is down because you are being entertained, and you uncritically absorb everything you see and hear. *Star Wars* does more than make money for George Lucas; it consciously promotes and popularizes a New Age view of God.

"Look to the East for wisdom," young people today are advised. For the East is considered a source of mystery and wisdom, personified by the stereotyped guru who sits filthy and half-naked on a mountaintop and does nothing but contemplate infinity and give obtuse and incomprehensible answers to those who so earnestly seek his advice.

For many centuries the West has sent missionaries to the East, but for the past several decades the East has evangelized the West. Back in the 60s it was "cool" for a college man to have a Buddha, amulet or other Oriental symbol (even if it was only a Jade East cologne bottle!) in his dorm room. The gods those symbols represented followed closely behind. And now, using the mechanism of the New Age movement, they are engaged in deadly battle for the heart and soul of America.

Western and Eastern thought have merged and diverged time and again throughout history. The essential difference between Western and Eastern thought is difficult to capsulize, but it probably can be best summarized in this observation: Western thought emphasizes the personal and the individual, while Eastern thought emphasizes the impersonal and the group.

In medieval times it was said that when a Western army and an Eastern army came together in battle, the goal of the Western army was to kill or disable the Eastern army's leader, because without a leader the Eastern army could not function. If the Westerners lost their king, the Western knights could carry on the fight as individuals; the Eastern warriors could not. This illustrates the difference between Western and Eastern thinking.

Historically in Europe and Asia, the further east one goes the more the individual is subordinated to society and the state. The further west one goes, the more the legal and political systems emphasizes limited decentralized government and individual rights. The early Anglo-Saxons governed themselves by decentralized authority; they placed a tithingman over every ten families, a vilman over every fifty families, a hundred-man over every hundred families, and an eolderman (later shortened to earl) over every thousand families. Norsemen applied Viking law in Scandinavia and other areas they ruled, a very localized, limited, individualistic form of government centered in the Althing, a local parliament and court in which every freeman participated as an equal. By contrast, in Eastern Europe individual rights were less pronounced, and in the oriental despotisms the individual was almost totally subordinated to the state.

And the most individualistic and adventuresome men and women of Europe went still further west — to America. And as Americans began settling the frontier, "Go west, young man" was the advice for individualistic young Americans. Even today, the West is still thought of as the last frontier of rugged individualism.

The same is true of Western and Eastern views of God. In Western thought, God is a person. That doesn't mean He has a physical body — that is true only of the Second Person of the Trinity, Jesus Christ. Rather, it means He has the qualities of personhood: will, intellect, emotion, and action.

The Old Testament sets forth the basic view of God for three primary Western religions: Judaism, Christianity, and to some extent Islam. In the Old Testament God is a distinct person. He has a definite and sovereign will; He has infinite intellect (omniscience); He has emotions; He acts in creation and in human history. In the New Testament, which Christians accept as the revelation of God, His personhood is defined still further as He becomes incarnate in human flesh in the Person of Jesus Christ.

The Eastern view of God is different. God is not thought of as a person, but rather as an impersonal force, a ground of being, an idea. Hinduism, Buddhism, Confucianism and other eastern religions generally see God in this way. While these religions often recognized the existence of gods, or spirits, or demons, these were lesser beings, subordinate to and part of the ultimate idea of

God. And this is the view of God in the New Age movement.

This idea has spread to the West. Some western intellectuals have been unwilling to accept the personal God of Scripture but have also been reluctant to take that full step toward atheism. They have found the Eastern concept of an impersonal God, a ground of being or idea or "Force," an uneasy middle ground position between Christianity and atheism. Sometimes without knowing it, they have looked to the East for wisdom.

A century ago, American society was formed around a Christian consensus. The Christian world view and Christian moral values were almost universally accepted, even if they were not always practiced. People learned about God through the Bible as it was taught to them at home, in school and at church.

Today that consensus has broken down somewhat. Partly because of the rise of secular and pagan elements in society, partly because of the breakdown of the family unit, partly because the Bible no longer occupies a prominent place in the schools, partly because many churches have watered down the Gospel, much of our population is unchurched and biblically illiterate.

That's why movies like *Star Wars* have such an impact upon people who are searching for truth and don't know where to find it. For millions of people who never darken the door of a church, go to movie theaters and absorb the *Star Wars* concept of God.

Remember the oft-repeated *Star Wars* benediction: "May the Force be with you!" God, in Stars Wars thought, is the same as in Eastern religions. He is not the personal God of Scripture, but rather He is reduced to the level of an impersonal "Force." Consider the words of the demon Screwtape in C.S. Lewis's famous work:

> If once we can produce our perfect work — the Materialist Magician, the man, not using, but veritably worshipping, what he vaguely calls "Forces" while denying the existence of "spirits" — then the end of the war will be in sight.[3]

And the *Screwtape Letters* were written over thirty years before the appearance of *Star Wars*.

Consider the matter further. Remember Darth Vader, the black-clad villain in *Star Wars*. Where did he derive his power? The "dark side of the Force!"

Here again we see an Eastern view of God and reality, that good an evil are two sides of the same coin. New Age thought, like Oriental philosophy, is a unique combination of monism and dualism.

Monism (in Latin "monos" means one) stresses the oneness or unity of everything. As Dr. Gary North says, monism teaches that "There is no Creator-creature distinction. We are all gods in the making. Out of One has proceeded the many, and back into One are the many travelling. ...in terms of monism, everything is valuable and holy in life or death, for there is no death.... Monism is the philosophy of nihilism [nothingness], however disguised it may be."₄

In contrast to monism is dualism (in Latin "duos" means two). Dualism divides the cosmos into two opposite categories, each balancing the other, each of approximately equal force, and both coexisting from eternity to eternity. Sometimes the division is good vs. evil, sometimes spirit vs. matter, sometimes male vs. female. The Orientals often conceptualized them as yang and yin in a diagram like this:

The Orientals also pictured a two-faced god, a god with one head but two faces, one representing good and one representing evil.

The New Age represents a combination of monism and dualism. In New Age thought good and evil, spirit and matter, maleness and femaleness all exist, but they are all aspects of one and the same ultimate reality. The Force has a bright or

good side to which Obi-Wan Kenobi and Yoda are
attuned, and a dark or evil side to which Darth
Vader is attuned. But they are two sides of the
same Force.

And how do we know good from evil? How do we
decide which side of the Force to serve? Yoda
offers Luke only enigmatic advice:

> "This will not do. Anger is what you feel. Anger,
> fear, aggression — the dark side of the Force. Easily
> they flow. Beware, beware, beware of them. A heavy
> price is paid for the power they bring."
> Luke lowered his saber. "Price? What do you mean?"
> "The dark side beckons. If you start down the dark
> path, forever will it dominate your destiny. Consume
> you it will, as it did Obi-Wan's apprentice."
> Luke nodded. "Vader. Then is the dark side stron-
> ger?"
> "No, no. Easier. Quicker. More seductive."
> "How am I to know the good side from the bad?"
> "You will know. When you are at peace. Calm. A
> Jedi uses the Force for knowledge and defense. Never
> for attack."
> "But why … "
> Yoda cut him off. "There is no why. Clear your mind
> of questions. Quiet now. Be … at peace …." Yoda's voice
> trailed off.[5]

At first this may sound like a Christian view.
But while Christianity certainly considers good
and evil to be opposites, it does not treat them as
equals. Dualism has been a heresy throughout
church history, best represented by the Manichean
view that treats God and Satan, good and evil, as
two roughly equal forces bitterly contesting for
mastery of the universe.

This conflict between God and Satan is certainly a central theme of Scripture, but they are far from equal. God is omnipotent (all-powerful), omniscient (all- knowing), omnipresent (present everywhere), and eternal (existing from before the beginning of time through and past the end of time). Satan is very powerful, very intelligent, and capable of traveling at great speed, but he is not omnipotent, omniscient, and omnipresent like God. And while he will live eternally in the Lake of Fire (Rev. 20:10), he was created by God at a point of time; he did not exist from eternity past the way God did.

Far from being an eternal conflict between good and evil as two roughly equal cosmic forces, evil in the biblical view is a rebellion within the system, a revolt by self-willed created beings against the God who created them. They are able to carry on their evil work for the present only because God in His longsuffering allows them to do so. But Revelation 19-22 leaves us with no doubt that God is and will be the total victor in this conflict!

Likewise Scripture totally rejects the *Star Wars* concept of the "Dark Side of the Force." Consider the words of 1 John 1:5: "This then is the message which we have heard of him, and declare unto you, that God is light, and in him is no darkness at all."

What could be clearer than that? God is total and complete righteousness. There is no sin or evil in Him, and consequently we cannot be in fellowship with Him if we have unconfessed sin in our lives. In short: There is no "Dark Side of the Force" with God!

And despite what Yoda says, we do not just "know" good from evil by feeling at peace with the Force and with ourselves. The *StarWars* approach is to turn off our minds, stop thinking, and follow whatever course our feelings tell us is in harmony with the Force.

But Scripture emphasizes that "There is a way which seemeth right unto a man, but the end thereof are the ways of death" (Prov. 14:12; 16:25). Our feelings, even our conscience, can deceive us. They are limited, and they can be manipulated by our own sin nature and the forces of evil. We learn right from wrong by carefully seeking the will of God through prayer and diligent study of His revealed Word.

POSTSCRIPT: As I type this manuscript, I am in a La Quinta Motel in Houston, Texas, where I am to lecture this evening. I am dividing my attention between this manuscript and a television movie, *Maid to Order*. The star of the show, a young, beautiful, but spoiled heiress named Jessica, winds up in jail, and her father says disgustedly, "I wish I'd never had a daughter."

The scene fades to the stars, one of which twinkles above all others; and in the next scene a blond woman comes to the jail, bails Jessica out, and informs her that she, Stella (Latin for "star"), is her fairy godmother, that her father's wish has just been granted and that Jessica's father and household are now under a spell whereby they do not recognize her. When she tries to return home, she is treated as an intruder and ejected by the police. Her fairy godmother advises her she will never be allowed to return home until she changes her attitude and makes something of her life.

Forced to get a job, she becomes a maid in a wealthy household and gradually learns humility, the value of hard work, and concern for others. As she and the other servants cater a lavish party at which her father is a guest, they look out over the party and express their wishes. A maid with unrecognized talent wishes to be a singing star; a chauffeur who composes songs wishes the crowd could hear his music; a cook wishes someone could clean up the kitchen for her that night; Jessica, though longing to return home, places others above herself and says resignedly, "I wish all of your wishes would come true."

Stella overhears this and arranges for it all to happen. As Stella demonstrates her occult power of mind over matter, she forces a coconut to fall from a palm tree onto the head of the chief entertainer for the evening. Since he is unable to sing, the maid takes his place that night, and sings the chauffeur's music, much to the delight of the crowd. A talent scout offers them both contracts, and they proceed to celebrate by cleaning up the kitchen for the cook.

As Stella watches approvingly, Jessica's father recognizes her as though she has never been gone, and he brings her home. Stella, the fairy godmother then prepares to depart. Jessica says, "I sort of thought you'd disappear in a bubble." But instead Stella says, "Get real! This is the twentieth century!" and steps into a late-model sports car and drives off into the sunset.

Thus our emotions are captured as occult powers are used for the good purposes of building character and granting everyone their wishes at the same time, while the occult view of the cosmos is adapted to the twentieth century in which sports cars replace bubbles and barges into *Mists of Avalon* as means of conveyance in and out of reality.

### ENDNOTES

1. *The StarWars Storybook* (New York: Scholastic Book Services, 1978).

2. *The Empire Strikes Back Storybook* (New York: Scholastic Book Services, 1980).

3. C.S. Lewis, *The Screwtape Letters* (New York: Macmillan, 1961, 1968), pp. 32-33.

4. Gary North, *Unholy Spirits: Occultism and New Age Deception* (Fort Worth: Dominion Press, 1986), p. 61.

5. *The Empire Strikes Back Storybook*, op. cit.

## CHAPTER FOUR

# GOD IS NATURE IS GOD

Most people divide the physical universe into two classes: organic and inorganic, or living and nonliving matter. Horses, cattle, dogs, cats, wolves, birds, fish, insects, flowers, grass, trees and the like are living things. Rocks, dirt, concrete, water, air, wind, rain, thunder, the earth, the moon, the sun, stars, comets, meteors, etc., are nonliving.

In the New Age view of reality, no such distinction exists. All matter is living, both physically and spiritually. As Daniel Cohen observes in *Curses, Hexes and Spells,*

> Another important principle to understand about magic is the magician's view of an animistic universe, that is, a universe that is alive. Practically everything you can name — people, animals, trees, rivers, rocks, the wind — have spirits. Sometimes these spirits are vague and undefined. Sometimes they are highly personal. By the use of his magic the magician seeks to use or control these forces.[1]

In this way, then, the New Age world view is like the old pagan world view, and very different from that of Secular Humanism. Secular Humanism

views the universe as material, with no room for
the supernatural. The New Age is the direct
opposite: Everything is supernatural. In the New
Age view, God permeates the entire universe — in
fact, God is one with the universe, and the universe
is God.

Some, however, insist that this difference is not
as significant as it appears. Some describe their
world view as "super natural," not supernatural.
That is, they believe the natural forces of the
universe are broader and more varied and perhaps
even more mystical than humanists and modern
scientists are willing to accept; but there is no
such thing, technically speaking, as supernatural
or spiritual reality. Mark Roberts, for example,
says there is less difference between "mortal" and
"deity" than there is between those who have lost
touch with nature and those whose rhythms and
pulse are attuned to the universe. He writes,

> The lifestyle of a Dianic [a member of a certain
> tradition of witchcraft named after Diana, the goddess
> of the hunt and the moon] is a composite of three values
> and ideals. First, an awareness of self. Second, an
> increasing and evergrowing kinship with Nature. And
> third, an open sensitivity to the pulsebeat of the
> cosmos. As we near the common goals of awareness,
> kinship, and sensitivity, we attain the level of
> attunement that outsiders call "magic." We are well
> aware that in our workings we have achieved and
> produced nothing supernatural; we have simply
> reached our level of natural capacity.[2]

In general, though, the New Age movement

views the earth not simply as a rocky planet on which various life forms make their homes. Rather, the earth herself is a living, vibrant organism, to be worshipped as God. So the earth is often capitalized as Planet Earth or Spaceship Earth, or the Earth Mother, or the Mother Goddess. A generation ago, "Mother Nature" was used as a euphemistic phrase for nature itself, but today that phrase is used with more reverence.

Many of the ancient pagans, such as the Druids of early England and Wales, worshipped the earth and its natural forces. While their beliefs and practices varied greatly, they generally regarded the Earth Mother as a feminine deity and underlying principle of all things. She is the fertility goddess, the underlying cause of all good harvests and productivity. She was worshipped as a goddess. Some of them also believed in a masculine god, sometimes referred to as the Horned God. Frequently there was an annual fertility ritual in which a chosen man of the community, embodying the spirit of the Horned God, mated with a chosen woman of the community, embodying the spirit of the Mother Goddess. Through this ritual pagans brought down to earth the fertility powers of the Horned God and the Mother Goddess and thereby helped to ensure a good harvest or a good hunting season.

The various pagan cultures worshipped forces of nature personified as gods. As a child I enjoyed mythology. Norse mythology especially fascinated me, probably because of my own Norwegian heritage. Odin was the All-Father, father of the gods. His wife was Frigg, the earth mother. Thor was the thunder-god, Tyr the god of fire, Freya the goddess of love and fertility, Balder the god of springtime, Heimdal the guardian of the gods, and so on.

Norse mythology was simply a variation of other cultures' myths. Odin was called Wotan by the Teutons, Lieu by the Celts, Jupiter by the Romans, Zeus by the Greeks, Baal by the Canaanites, Marduk by the Babylonians, and Nimrod by the Sumerians. As cultures proliferated, variations occurred. Living in the land of glaciers and the midnight sun, the Norse invented myths of frost giants which figured prominently in the battles against the gods; the Greeks and Babylonians, living in the southland, gave little thought to frost giants. But the pantheon of gods is remarkably similar from one culture to the next.

As a child I used to wonder, did my Viking ancestors really believe in such characters as Thor, Odin and Loki? Did the Norse believe them to be real, or did they merely tell them as stories, mainly for fun, partially to teach a moral principle?

The answer is that in the pagan mind it doesn't matter whether they are "real," as we would use the term. Remember, in pagan thought as in New Age thought, perception is reality. What matters is whether Thor and Odin are real *to you*. If you believe in them, they become real in your scheme of things. And that is all that really matters.

In comparing this New Age view of God/Nature to the Christian view of God, we must bear in mind the terms "immanence" and "transcendence." In theological terms, immanence (not to be confused with imminence, which means soon to happen) means that God is present within His creation and is identified with nature. Like most pagan religions, in the New Age view God is immanent rather than transcendent.

Transcendence means that God is above and beyond nature. Deism, the belief that God created the universe and established laws by which the universe operates but subsequently withdrew from the universe and is no longer involved with man or the universe, is the ultimate form of transcendence.

Christianity teaches that God is both transcendent and immanent. Being omnipresent, He is present in His creation. "Do I not fill heaven and earth? saith the Lord." (Jer. 23:24) But over and above that, He is primarily transcendent. He is infinitely greater than His creation.

The Christian appreciates nature, but he does not worship nature. In nature the Christian sees the handiwork of God. The Psalmist says, "The heavens are telling the glory of God, and the firmament showeth His handiwork. Day unto day uttereth speech, and night unto night showeth forth knowledge"(Ps. 19:1-2). The Christian sees God in nature, and he learns about God through nature. Through creation the Christian sees God's power, His orderliness, His design, His beauty, His constancy, His majesty, His attention to detail, His infinite variety. But while the Christian sees God in creation and worships God through creation, he knows that the Creator is infinitely greater than His creation. God is in nature, but nature is not God.

Viewing God as immanent rather than transcendent has profound implications for worship and for life.

The biblical view, then, is that God is in nature but also above nature. We do not become one with Him by going back to nature or following our natural instincts. Rather, we become His children through trusting Jesus Christ and His death on the Cross to cleanse us from all sin, and then, through the power of the Holy Spirit and as the result of salvation, we conform our lives to His will and His character as revealed in His Word.

## ENDNOTE

1. Daniel Cohen, *Curses Hexes, and Spells* (Philadelphia: J.B. Lippincott Company, 1974), pp. 98-100.

2. Mark Roberts, quoted by Margot Adler, *Drawing Down the Moon* (Boston: Beacon Press, 1979, 1986), pp. 122-23.

## CHAPTER FIVE

# EVOLUTION: MAN'S LINK WITH NATURE

Evolution is a central tenet of New Age thought.

Evolution is also a central feature of Humanist thought, but for different reasons. As Humanist Manifesto II declares, " ... science affirms that the human species is an emergence from natural evolutionary forces."[1]

Evolution is the belief that life gradually developed from lower to higher forms over a long period of time. But it is also a philosophy and world view. The philosophy of evolution sees a world in flux, a universe of constant change, a cosmos without moral or physical absolutes.

It sees man as a product of environmental determinism. In practically every academic discipline, currently prevailing theories have their roots in evolutionary thought. Both Freudian and Jungian psychology are based upon evolutionary principles, Freudianism being more consistent with Humanism and Jungianism more compatible with the New Age. Progressive Deweyite educational theory is based upon the premise that man is a product of evolution. Anthropology views man as an evolutionary product and consequently regards primitive cultures as similar to what the rest of us once were. The same can be said of the study of history, language, literature, and practically every field of thought. Karl Marx wanted to dedicate the English version of *Das Capital* to Darwin, declaring that Darwin's concept of survival of the fittest had provided a biological basis for the class struggle (Darwin, however, refused this "honor")[2], while at the same time many American industrialists used Darwin's concept of survival of the fittest to justify their tooth- and-claw version of capitalism.[3]

For the Humanist, evolution is more than a scientific model of origins. It fills a vital role in Humanist philosophy, for it enables the Humanist to declare his independence from God. So long as man believes in a creator God, he must outwardly acknowledge that a creature cannot be greater than his Creator. This sobering realization forces him, intellectually at least, to kneel before the throne of God. Evolution gives man an explanation of origins that does not require belief in God — not a satisfactory explanation, but an explanation nevertheless.

Like the Humanist, the New Age thinker believes in evolution as a religious tenet. Like the Humanist, the New Ager uses evolution to explain man's origins. But unlike the Humanist, the New Ager uses evolution to explain man's present position in the universe, and also to explain man's destiny.

The Bible teaches that God created man in His image (Gen. 1:27; 9:6), that He gave man dominion over nature (Gen. 1:28, 9:1-5), and that He created man with a spirit by which man can commune with God. Thus while God designed man with a physical structure in some ways similar to that of animals, He created man distinct from animals. Nowhere does the Bible say that any animal was created in the image of God. Never was an animal given dominion over the earth. And while the Bible does speak of animals as having souls, nowhere does the Bible say any animal has a spirit. No animal has the ability that man has to commune and have fellowship with God.

The biblical view of man is thus diametrically opposed to the New Age view of man. In the biblical view, man is distinct from nature and has dominion over nature. In the New Age view, man has evolved through nature and is therefore part of nature. He and the animals are all one big family, and even the plants are distant cousins. The New Ager thus feels a oneness with nature that the Christian does not; at the same time, the Christian appreciates God through nature in a way the New Ager cannot.

Partially for this reason, those who are deeply concerned about ecology often are attracted to the New Age movement. The idea that man is one with nature lends itself naturally to an emphasis on ecology. One New Age writer even says the current environmental pollution crisis is a direct result of the Earth Mother resisting and throwing off the Christian God and the dominion mandate He is wrongfully supposed to have given to man over the earth.

For this reason, too, New Agers often tend to be vegetarian. Some claim vegetarian animals are more highly developed on the evolutionary scale than carnivores. Others argue that the human digestive system is not really designed for eating meat. Still others consider meat-eating to be almost like cannibalism, because animals are related to us. As the head of People for the Ethical Treatment of Animals declares, "There is no rational basis for saying that a human being has special rights. A rat is a pig is a dog is a boy."[4] (Apparently vegetables are far enough removed on the family tree that eating them is morally acceptable.)

Note, however, that God expressly authorized man to eat meat:

> Every moving thing that liveth shall be meat for you; even as the green herb have I given you all things (Gen. 9:3).

Jesus Christ, whom Christians regard as Lord

and Savior and whom most in the New Age call a great guru or spirit guide, gave His disciples bread and meat at the Last Supper and fed the five thousand loaves and fishes. He himself is described at mealtime as being "at meat" (Mark 14:3). Jesus Christ is the world's foremost authority on the human digestive system, because as the Creator God He designed it (John 1:1, 3, 14; Col. 1:13-16; Heb. 1:1-3). Since our Lord loved mankind so much that He was willing to die for the sin of the world, it seems unlikely that He would give us food that is not good for us.

Like Humanism, the New Age regards evolution as an upward process. Animals and plants are evolving into better animals and plants. Better animals and plants are "higher" on the evolutionary scale than others. Fish are a higher form of life than amoebas; reptiles are higher than fish; mammals are higher than reptiles; apes are the highest form of animal life, and man is the most highly evolved ape. But what makes one animal or plant "higher" or "better" than others? The answer is *consciousness,* or awareness of oneself and one's surroundings. Animals are more conscious than plants; reptiles are more conscious than insects (or so we think); apes are more conscious than reptiles; and man is the most highly conscious organism of all.

And in the New Age view, evolution is a continuing process. Man is currently the most highly evolved, most highly conscious organism, but he is in the process of evolving toward a still higher form of life. This evolutionary process is usually gradual, taking millions and millions of years. But sometimes it takes place in leaps and bounds, a view growing in acceptance by modern scientists (largely because of the lack of fossil evidence for gradual transitional forms) and known as punctuated equilibrium.

And mankind, New Agers say, is on the verge of a great "quantum leap" of evolution — toward the new Aquarian race of the future, a race that will have a much higher consciousness than ours.

This new Aquarian race, we are told will be blessed with "corporate consciousness"; that is, the entire race will think together as one organism. To illustrate what I mean, your body is composed of many organs, but you think as one organism. Your heart doesn't have one thought, your liver another, your right lung still another, etc. You think as one corporate organism. After this quantum evolutionary leap into the new Aquarian race, the whole race will think as one corporate organism. Mary Smith won't be thinking one isolated thought, and Bill Jones another; we will all think one corporate thought. I can think of nothing more ghastly, more repulsive, more destructive of privacy, individualism, and the personal life, than this. But then, as we saw in Chapter Two, the New Age stresses the impersonal above the personal, the group above the individual.

In the meantime, the human race remains the most highly conscious portion of the animal family. And man is, or should be, steadily working to elevate or enhance his consciousness. That, in a nutshell, is what this existence is all about.

The New Age hope, then, is not in the Lord Jesus Christ who died for our sins and has prepared a place for us in heaven with God. Rather, the New Age hope is the evolving consciousness which will lead eventually to a new and better race and a new and better world.

But this life is not all there is. The process of evolving consciousness continues after death. Most New Agers believe in reincarnation, the idea that after death man will be reborn into another life. Some even believe that in our next life we will get to choose who our parents are, where we live, etc. (Note: When you combine this concept of reincarnation with the current "death education" courses which teach high school students that "suicide is your right," etc., is it any wonder that teen suicide is as high as it is?)

The idea of reincarnation is not new. Is has its roots in Hindu thought in which reincarnation is a central feature. But while Western New Agers see reincarnation as their hope for eternal life, to the Hindus reincarnation is not a blessing, but rather a curse. It is part of the age-old law of "karma," the idea that man must be reincarnated to pay for past sins. Karma teaches that man reaps what he sows, and our bad deeds come back to haunt us in future lives. If you live an evil life, next time around you might be reincarnated as a lowly animal; if you live well, your next life might be a step upward on the evolutionary scale. In the Eastern view man is trapped in this endless cycle of death and reincarnation — hardly a joyful prospect! His only hope is Nirvana, which Westerners sometimes equate with heaven but which is really more like oblivion or nothingness.

In the Christian view, reincarnation is neither a blessing nor a curse. It is nonexistent. Scripture says, "It is appointed unto a man once to die, but after this the judgment" (Heb. 9:27). We live on earth but once.

But Scripture also provides hope. Those who want to be saved can find their salvation through the Lord Jesus Christ. God became man in the Person of Jesus Christ and died for the sin of the world. We need not face the judgment of God, because Christ paid the penalty for us. For those who trust Him, He provides salvation from sin and eternal life in heaven with Him.

> For God so loved the world that He gave His only begotten Son, that whosoever believeth on Him should not perish but have everlasting life (John 3:16).

### ENDNOTES

1. "Humanist Manifesto II," reprinted in *Hu-*

*manist Manifestos I and I* (Buffalo, New York: Prometheus Books,1973, 1978), pp. 16-17.

2. *Encyclopedia Brittanica: Macropaedia Knowledge In Depth*, 15th Ed., s.v. "Darwin, Charles,," by Sir Gavin DeBeer, 5:495. See also, Sir Gavin DeBeer, *Charles Darwin* (London: Thomas Nelson & Sons, Ltd., 1963), p. 266.

3. For a detailed discussion of the evolutionary views of Andrew Carnagey, John D. Rockefeller, James Jerome Hill, and others, see John Eidsmoe, *The Christian Legal Advisor* (Grand Rapids, Michigan: Baker Book House, 1984, 1987), pp. 68-69.

4. Stephen Chapman, "The Radical Animal Rights Crusaders," *Valley Morning Star* [Harlingen, Texas], December 5, 1989, p. A4.

*CHAPTER SIX*

# MAN IS GOD IS MAN

If you've been following the logic of the last two chapters, the next step is obvious. Nature is God. Man is an evolutionary outgrowth of nature. Therefore, man is God.

Thirty years ago, if a person claimed that he was God, people thought he was either a con artist or mentally disturbed. But today the idea that man is God is taken seriously.

It isn't always expressed quite that bluntly, of course. Some prefer to speak of the "God within us," or "developing one's innate potential for godhood," or "the divine spark that indwells every human being." But the basic concept is the same: Man is God.

The thought is not new. It was Lucifer's thought when he rebelled against God: "I will be like the most High" (Isa.14:14). And he tempted Eve with the same thought: "Ye shall be as gods ..." (Gen. 3:5).

During the Middle Ages, a cult arose at the University of Paris that taught that man is God. As Jeffrey Burton Russell explains,

... a scholar named Amalric of Bena (d. 1206), under
the influence of the writings of John Scotus Eriugena,
taught an intellectually refined form of pantheism,
asserting that "God is all things in all things." About
1190 an Italian named Joachim of Flora enunciated a
millenarian theology: there were three ages of the
world — that of the Father, that of the Son, and that of
the Holy Spirit. The last he predicted would come in
1260 and would revolutionize the world, bringing the
Kingdom of God into the hearts of men. The first age
had been the rule of law, the second age was the rule
of faith, but the third age was an age in which God
would reveal himself directly to each man. Since all
men would be transformed by God, there would be no
need for law, governments, or the Church; there would
be no need even for food, for men's bodies would be
spiritually transformed. Seeing God face to face, men
would spend their lives in endless joy.

The pantheism of Amalric and the hopeful
millenarianism of Joachim were combined from about
1205 to about 1230 in the doctrine of a group called the
Amalricians who, unlike the professor from whom
they derived their name, were largely unlettered. If
God is all things, they argued, then I am God, unable
to sin. I can do wrong only when I forget that I am God.
They advanced the date for the coming of the Third Age
to 1210, presumably so that they could be assured of
enjoying it themselves. At that time, they said, all men
would be converted to their sect, outside of which there
could be no salvation.[1]

And today there is a neo-pagan group called the
Church of All Worlds. The members greet each
other with the salutation, "Thou art God" or
"Thou art Goddess."[2]

So man is God because nature is God and man
is part of nature. But it is more than that. Man has

realized his "godhood" more than the rest of nature, because man has the most highly evolved consciousness of any being of nature. More than any other animal, man is aware of his surroundings, aware of his place with the rest of nature, aware of the problems facing our world and thus able to do something about them. New Agers even conduct "consciousness-raising" seminars to heighten people's awareness of the environment, world peace, or whatever issue they are concerned about.

Modern psychology is one field in which this man-is-God philosophy is taken seriously. Much of modern psychology is based upon the theories of Freud, who considered religion to be a neurosis of mankind in which the concept of God is a fictitious extension of the human father idea as a refuge from fear. Karl Jung, who has probably influenced psychology more than any other person except Freud, had a lifelong interest in superstition, mythology, and the occult. He taught that the members of every race share a deep level of unconsciousness, which he called the "collective unconscious." Within this collective unconscious are archetypes or primordial patterns of human types, and that the gods and supernatural powers of mythology are part of and expressions of this collective unconscious. He believed this collective unconscious contains a pool of human wisdom that guides all humanity. Part of the role of

psychotherapy, he thought, was to bring people
into contact with this collective subconscious.[3]
From this, it is just another step of reasoning to
say that this collective subconscious is the mind of
God (or Goddess, or Earth Mother) that is in all of
us.

I am not making a blanket condemnation of all
holistic healing, but much of that movement is
based upon New Age concepts. Central to much of
holistic healing is the idea that there is an energy
field within each person that is part of a universal
"energy field," that knows all things and is capable
of doing all things. It is sometimes known by other
names, such as Chi, vital force, bioenergy,
bioplasmic, prana (yoga), Kundalini (evolutionary
energy), and life force.[4] Much of holistic healing,
then, is directed toward making that energy field
flow freely within you so you can fully make use
of its power and knowledge. Because of the Western
belief in a transcendent and personal God,
Westerners are less likely to explicitly connect the
energy field with God; but Eastern thinkers and
practitioners are much less hesitant to do so. In
fact, it is through the energy field that all things
are united into one. The concept of the energy
field thus becomes a central feature of New Age
monism.

Incredible though it may seem, the "Man-is-
God" philosophy is taken seriously even in some
Christian circles. One leading charismatic evan-

gelist has told his television audience, "You are God!." Then he added, "Note that I did not say you have God living within you; I said you are God!" I do not choose to identify this evangelist because I consider him to be a believer in Jesus Christ and I do not wish to divide the Christian community by publicly attacking a fellow Christian. But this Christian man and those who follow him in this teaching are on dangerous ground!

New Age advocates are likely to quote Scripture to prove their point. Believing that all paths lead to God, and knowing that Western culture is based upon the Bible, New Agers see the Bible as a useful tool to sell their beliefs to a Western audience. And doesn't the Apostle Paul tell us that "Christ liveth in me" (Gal. 2:19)? Isn't that saying the same thing as the New Age movement — I am God?

Not at all! There is all the difference in the world between saying Christ lives in me, and saying I am Christ or I am God. Since I am a believer in Christ, He does dwell in me, and if you are a believer He dwells in you. But I am not Jesus Christ, and I will never become Jesus Christ. While I hope to grow in sanctification and reflect a small portion of His righteousness, justice and love, I will never possess His sovereignty, omnipotence, omniscience, and omnipresence. And neither will you!

In the West, New Age cults like to identify

themselves with Jesus Christ, for this gains them
acceptance and respectability among American
audiences. But their view of Jesus Christ is incomplete and erroneous. Some speak of Him as
our adult brother, great teacher, or spirit guide.
Others consider Him the Son of God, but not fully
equal with the Father. Many New Age cultists,
when asked whether or not they believe in Christ,
answer without explanation or questions, "Yes!"
because that is the popular answer in Western
culture. But they define Him differently from the
way orthodox Christians define Him, regarding
Him simply as a great teacher or doer of good
deeds. He was all of that, but He is more: He is the
immortal and eternal Son of God! Many will even
answer that they believe in Jesus as the Son of
God, but they define the term differently. They
mean Jesus is a great guru or spirit guide who has
evolved farther than anyone else toward godhood.
But we are evolving toward godhood too, and
someday we will be as far advanced toward
godhood as Jesus is now — only by then He will be
further evolved yet! For that is what life is all
about, a constant upward process of evolution
toward godhood.

To separate the New Age cultist from the orthodox Christian, it is best to ask the question
this way: "Do you believe in Jesus Christ as the
Second Person of the Trinity, fully equal with God
the Father and God the Holy Spirit in every

respect?" If the New Age cultist is being honest with you, he will have to answer "No" to that question.

## ENDNOTES

1. Jeffrey Burton Russell, *Witchcraft In The Middle Ages* (Ithaca, New York: Cornell University Press, 1972), pp. 138- 39.

2. Margot Adler, *Drawing Down the Moo* (Boston: Beacon Press, 1979, 1986), p. 310.

3. *The World Book Encyclopedia*, 1985 ed., s.v. "Jung, Carl Gustav;" s.v. "Freud, Sigmund;" see also *Lutheran Cyclopedia* (St. Louis: Concordia, 1954, 1975), s.v. "Freud," "Jung," "Psychology," "Psychotherapy."

4. Jane D. Gumprecht, M.D., *Holistic Health; A Medical and Biblical Critique Of New Age Deception* (Moscow, Idaho: Ransom Press, 1986), pp. 52-3.

CHAPTER SEVEN

# WE CREATE OUR OWN REALITY

The various tenets of New Age theology now start to come together, and what seems at first to be a disjointed and confused movement comes into focus as a somewhat consistent and systematic way of looking at the world.

There are no absolute moral values and no absolute reality. God and man are impersonal. Nature is God. Man is an evolutionary part of nature, and therefore man is God, the most highly evolved conscious being in nature.

Who is the creator of all reality? Who is the author of all morals, all values, all law? For the orthodox Christian, the obvious answer is God.

But as we saw in the last chapter, in the New Age view man is God. Therefore man can create his own reality!

You will recall from Chapter One that the basic underlying premise of New Age epistemology is that perception is reality. That is, ultimate reality is what we perceive it to be, and nothing else.

There is no objective reality "out there;" reality is in your mind and nowhere else. Therefore, you can control reality and create your own reality, simply by controlling your own mind.

Sylva Mind Control, for example, teaches basic techniques for controlling one's mind. It is based on the premise that the brain works according to vibrations of various frequencies. The average person's brain functions most of his waking hours at the beta level, which is about twenty vibrations per second. But the brain functions, for most purposes, most efficiently at the alpha brain wave level of seven to fourteen vibrations per second. Sylva Mind Control therefore works at developing relaxation techniques, etc., by which you can control your brainwaves, lower their frequency to alpha level and thus function more efficiently. Sylva also teaches that the brain is divided into right and left hemispheres, the "right brain" dealing with form and shape, art and music, imagination, creativity and intuition, the "left brain" dealing with language, logic, abstract reasoning, and analytical thinking. Sylva claims to be able to integrate the right brain and left brain so they work together. Another basic premise of Sylva Mind Control is that perception controls reality:

> Many people are beginning to realize that the mental
> pictures you put into your biocomputer brain affect

your body, your performance and your health.

Athletes are now training themselves for greater skills and endurance by picturing themselves playing the perfect game, running the perfect race. When the amateur tees up on the golf course and takes a furtive look at the water hazard to the left, then the wooded rough to the right, he has just programmed himself for a poorly-aimed drive. The professional, by seeing only the flag at the hole, programs himself for the straight drive.[1]

Treating the brain almost like a computer, Sylva Mind Control then teaches how to cancel negative thoughts, replace them with positive thoughts, and reprogram yourself at the alpha level.

The *Encyclopedia Of Self-Improvement,* a series of several 12-tape audiocassette albums, contains many practical suggestions for succeeding in business and in life itself. But it is based entirely upon self-help; help from God is never considered. The narrator claims, authoritatively and persuasively but utterly without proof, that it is a "universal law of nature" that you must become that which you think. The encyclopedia stresses financial success in particular. The message is repeated over and over again: "If you want to be rich, you have to think rich." As a corollary, the harder you concentrate upon being rich, the sooner you will become rich. To help yourself concentrate upon being rich, associate with rich people, travel in rich neighborhoods, wear expensive clothes, etc. The only problem is that if an ordinary person like me spends money like a rich person, he doesn't become rich; he quickly winds up in the poorhouse or jail![2]

This *Encyclopedia Of Self-Improvement* repeatedly quotes the biblical admonition, "As he thinketh in his heart, so is he" (Prov. 23:7). This is taken way out of context. The passage means that a man cannot be clean and upright on the outside but corrupt and sinful on the inside, because one's inner thoughts ultimately will manifest themselves in actions. The Bible does not imply that man can bring things into reality simply by thinking about them.

Throughout this nation, businesses and governmental agencies are being sold on New Age methods of enhancing the performance of their employees. Usually these businessmen are not dedicated to New Age thought; they are driven by the profit motive and are led to believe that these techniques will improve employee performance and thus enhance profits or productivity. The success motivation techniques are generally based upon the premise that we will become what we think. To become successful, then, we must first "think success."

The way to "think success" is through "visualization." Visualization is the process of picturing the desired goal: picture yourself closing the business deal, or getting the promotion, or winning that dream vacation, or driving that new Lincoln Continental, or moving into that luxury home.

Visualization is becoming a popular concept in many aspects of our world today. Shakti Gawain, in her book *Creative Visualization,* explains it simply: "Creative visualization is the technique of using your imagination to create what you want in your life."[3] She adds,

> In creative visualization you use your imagination to create a clear image of something you wish to manifest. Then you continue to focus on the idea or picture regularly, giving it positive energy until it becomes objective reality ... in other words, until you actually achieve what you have been visualizing.
>
> Creative visualization is magic in the truest and highest meaning of the word. It involves understanding and aligning yourself with the natural principles that govern the workings of our universe, and learning to use these principles in the most conscious and creative way.[4]

While she claims it is not necessary to believe in any metaphysical or spiritual ideas to practice creative visualization[5], her basis for visualization is very different from that of traditional Western thought:

> Our physical universe is not really composed of any "matter" at all; its basic component is a kind of force or essence which we call energy.
>
> Things appear to be solid and separate from one another on the level at which our physical senses normally perceive them. On finer levels, however,

atomic and subatomic levels, seemingly solid matter is
seen to be smaller and smaller particles within particles,
which eventually turn out to be just pure energy.

Physically, we are all energy, and everything within
and around us is made up of energy. We are all part of
one great energy field. Things which we perceive to be
solid and separate are in reality just various forms of
our essential energy which is common to all. We are all
one, even in a literal, physical sense.

The energy is vibrating at different rates of speed,
and thus has different qualities, from finer to denser.
Thought is a relatively fine, light form of energy and
therefore very quick and easy to change. Matter is
relatively dense, compact energy, and therefore slower
to move and change. Within matter there is great
variation as well. Living flesh is relatively fine, changes
quickly, and is easily affected by many things. A rock
is a much denser form, slower to change and more
difficult to affect. Yet even rock is eventually changed
and affected by the fine, light energy of water, for
example. All forms of energy are interrelated and can
affect one another.[6]

Note that Gawain has presented these propo-
sitions as dogmatic statements of fact, utterly
devoid of scientific evidence or any other form of
proof. But she has said nothing new. This was the
view of medieval alchemy — the highest form of
science of its day — the belief that through the
force of one's mental energy upon matter forms,
one can change one form of matter to another,
such as iron to gold.

Ms. Gawain continues, again without proof:
"One law of energy is this: energy of a certain
quality or vibration tends to attract energy of a

similar quality and vibration.">[7] Back in the 60s, when two people were unexplainably attracted to one another, we used to say they had good "vibes" for one another. I might say of someone who thinks like I do, "He's on my wave length."

She then expounds another "law" of energy:

> Thought is a quick, light, mobile form of energy. It manifests itself instantaneously, unlike the denser forms such as matter.
>
> When we create something, we always create it first in a thought form. A thought or idea always precedes manifestation. ...
>
> The idea is like a blueprint; it creates an image of the form, which then magnetizes and guides the physical energy to flow into that form and eventually manifests itself on the physical plane.
>
> The same principle holds true even if we do not take direct physical action to manifest our ideas. Simply having an idea or thought, holding it in your mind, is an energy which will tend to attract and create that form on the material plane. If you constantly think of illness, you eventually become ill; if you believe yourself to be beautiful, you will become so.[8]

Then Ms. Gawain explains the "law" of radiation and attraction:

> This is the principle that whatever you put out into the universe will be reflected back to you. "As you sow, so shall you reap."
>
> What this means from a practical standpoint is that we always attract into our lives whatever we think about the most, believe in most strongly, expect on the deepest levels, and/or imagine most vividly.[9]

Again, these "laws" are based on a New Age
world view and are presented utterly without
proof. We have already seen that psychology is
greatly influenced by New Age thinking. It is
therefore not surprising that visualization has
become a key tool of many psychologists and
psychiatrists today. One means of overcoming
trauma from bad experiences of the past is to
visualize those events from a different standpoint;
in the visualized recreation of the event, one is
victorious over the danger, or the supposed danger turns out to be benign, or someone comes in
and helps. One school of psychology even has its
patients visualize themselves being reborn, that
is, going through the birthing process in a pleasant
way in which the traumas of birth and infancy are
avoided.

The same is true in other fields of the health
profession. A holistic health practitioner may tell
his patient to visualize those broken bones coming together, or that wound healing, or those
painful sinuses becoming clear. In the view of
many, this will cause the healing by itself; others
will not go that far, but will say that it will help
speed the healing process.

Like many other aspects of the New Age
movement, visualization is practiced even in
Christian circles. The so-called "prosperity gospel"
and its adherents seem to be especially vulnerable to this type of thinking. Part of the process of

naming and claiming what God has promised us, according to this viewpoint, is to visualize it and concentrate upon it. As we do so, God will grant us that which we have named and claimed through visualization. This leads to prayer, meditation, visualization and concentration techniques similar to those used in business seminars or modern psychology, but with a chocolate coating of Christianity. Christians visualize themselves as becoming rich, or being healed of disease, or having their broken marriages put back together, or just being happy.

Some Christian leaders who teach visualization are remarkably similar to their secular or New Age counterparts. One well-known Christian teacher, a leading advocate of healing through faith and prayer, says simply,

> The idea behind inner healing is simply that we can ask Jesus Christ to walk back to the time we were hurt and to free us from the effects of that wound in the present.[9]

Another Christian leader who is known throughout the world says,

> We should always try to visualize the end result as we pray ... If you have not visualized clearly in your own heart exactly what you hope for, it cannot become a reality to you. ...
>
> We have taught our people how to ... visualize success ... Through visualizing and dreaming, you can incubate your future and hatch the results.[10]

From a Christian standpoint, this is dangerous for several reasons: (1) It leads people to believe God has promised things which He has not promised; (2) It leads to disillusionment when the promised things do not materialize as expected; people think that either God has not lived up to His promises or we have failed Him by not exercising the necessary faith, using the right techniques, etc.; (3) It leads to an obsession with material blessing; (4) It causes people to lose sight of the fact that God often gives us His greatest blessings through tragedy and adversity; indeed, it is through these that we often have our greatest growth; (5) It gives Satan and his demons the opportunity to confuse believers and lead them astray by giving us that which we have requested of God; (6) It can cause people to lose their industry and initiative and depend upon visualization to get what God wants them to work for; and (7) It can lead people to believe the results were obtained by their own powers of visualization, rather than by the sovereign act of God.

There might be a good sense in which the term could be used. For example, if I want to get into better physical shape, I can picture myself as a human dynamo, with a few inches subtracted from the waist and hips and added to the chest and biceps instead. If that mental picture gives me the added drive and determination to run that extra mile, do those ten extra push-ups, and skip that chocolate dessert, great! But if I think that just by visualizing myself like that I can cause my body to conform itself to that visualized image, that's New Age thinking and it's both wrong and dangerous!

Modern New Age or neo-pagan cults use visualization even beyond the techniques described above. Part of the power behind curses, hexes, spells and incantations is the concentrated and visualized imagery or mental power behind it. Through the power of visualization many in the New Age believe they can actually conjure up spirit beings, or cause their own souls or "astral bodies" to travel through space, or even change the physical shape of their bodies to become animals or other creatures.

Some even apply visualization retroactively to create folklore or tradition for themselves. Many who are followers of a recently deceased neo-pagan leader from England named Gerald B. Gardner have tried to create their own mythology and ritual. Calling themselves Gardnerian witches, their lore is based upon English culture. Still others base their traditions upon Norse culture and mythology, or that of Greece, or that of Egypt, or that of various American Indian tribes, or whatever else they choose.[11]

Do they take this lore seriously? Do they actually believe these gods and rituals are real? If you have to ask questions like these, you have missed the basic point. For perception is reality! All that matters in New Age thought is that these things are real in their minds.

The problem with this type of thinking is that objective reality does exist, and it affects us and impacts upon us whether we accept it and believe in it or not. No one can practice New Age concepts of reality and stay alive for a week!

Suppose I stop for gas at a convenience store, and I purchase a can of Valvoline Motor Oil and a can of Dr. Pepper. I could ask the attendant, "Excuse me, Sir, but should I drink the Dr. Pepper and put the oil in the tank, or should I drink the oil and put the Dr. Pepper in the tank?" If the attendant happens to be a psychology major at a nearby university, he might answer, "Well, tell me, Sir, how do you *feel* about it?" It doesn't matter how I "feel" about it! Dr. Pepper is bad for my oil tank, and Valvoline is bad for my stomach, whether I feel good about it or not!

Or suppose I come to an intersection and wonder, "Is anything coming from the right? If I don't bother to look, whatever is there won't be in my scheme of reality, so it can't really be there and it can't hurt me." I assure you, if a truck is coming from the right, regardless of whether I see it, it will quickly become part of my scheme of reality, if only for a final, fatal second!

The point is, objective reality does exist, whether we wish to recognize it or not. And God's eternal standards of right and wrong exist regardless of whether we accept them. Proverbs 14:34 assures us, "Righteousness exalteth a nation: but sin is a reproach to any people." Those nations which violate God's standards of right and wrong will incure His judgment.

## ENDNOTES

1. Hans DeJong, *How To Use the Sylva Mind Control Method*, album of 2 audiotapes (Los Angeles: Audio Renaissance Tapes, Inc., 1989). See, also, the "Interactive Workbook" that goes with the tape album, especially pages 3, 5, 7-8, 11-14.

2. M.R. Kopmeyer, *Encyclopedia Of Self-Improvement*, Vol. Four: *Here's Help To Get Ride Of Problems And Fulfill Your Desires* (Louisville, Kentucky: The Success Foundation, Inc., 12 audiotapes, n.d.

3. Shakti Gawain, *Creative Visualization* (San Rafael, California: New World Library, 1978), p. 13.

4. Ibid., pp. 14-16.

5. Ibid., p. 15.

6. Ibid., pp. 17-18.

7. Ibid., p. 18.

8. Ibid., p. 19.

9. Dave Hunt and T.A. McMahon, *The Seduction Of Christianity* (Eugene, Oregon: Harvest House, 1985), p. 183.

10. Ibid., p. 145.

ll. See generally, Margot Adler, *Drawing Down the Moon* (Boston: Beacon Press, 19790, 1986), pp. 60-66, 78-85.

## CHAPTER EIGHT

# THE NEW AGE GOAL: BACK TO NATURE

New Age theology parallels Christian theology in some respects. Both teach that man has fallen from his original state, and both offer a way of salvation.

The Bible teaches that man was originally created in an ideal state, and that he originally lived without sin in an ideal environment, the Garden of Eden. But he chose to sin by rebelling against God and disobeying God. As a result he was expelled from the Garden of Eden, and is forced to earn his living from the earth. The curse applies not just to man but to all creation: "Cursed is the ground for thy sake," God says to Adam and Eve (Gen. 3:17). "Thorns and thistles shall it bring forth for thee. By the sweat of thy brow shalt thou toil and earn bread all the days of thy life; for dust thou art, and unto dust thou shalt return." And Paul reminds us that "The whole creation groaneth and travaileth in pain together until now" (Rom. 8:22). Sin originated with Satan, and he tempted

Eve and Adam; from them sin has spread like a cancer through all creation. As a result the earth is not the perfect environment it once was; instead of bountiful harvests with minimal effort we have unceasing toil, rewarded by crop failures, pestilences, weeds, and scarcities. Most of all, man is unable to have fellowship with God, because while God continues to love mankind, He is a God of righteousness and He will not tolerate sin in his presence. And it all goes back to the fact that man listened to Satan and disobeyed God.

In a sense, the New Ager too sees the problem in terms of man's estrangement from God. But in the New Age view, nature is God, and the problem is man's alienation from nature. Sin is not the reason; the New Age movement does not believe in sin, at least not in any traditional biblical sense of the term. As Shakti Gawain explains, "The truth about this earth is that it is an infinitely good, beautiful, nourishing place to be. The only 'evil' comes from lack of understanding of this truth. Evil (ignorance) is like a shadow — it has no real substance of its own, it is simply a lack of light. You cannot cause a shadow to disappear by trying to fight it, stamp on it, by railing against it, or any other form of emotional or physical resistance. In order to cause a shadow to disappear, you must shine light on it."[1]

Rather, the problem is lack of consciousness about the environment, or overpopulation, or modern technology, or a failure to recognize (consciousness again!) that we are all part of a global ecological community. Some even say the problem is traditional Christians who believe they have been created separate and distinct from nature instead of having evolved through nature. One New Age writer has even suggested that the current environmental crisis is the Earth Mother rejecting and throwing off the mandate that the Judeo- Christian God gave to man to exercise dominion over the earth. Some say man's vibrations are out of synchronism with the vibrations of Mother Nature.

Just as Christianity and the New Age both see the problem as man's estrangement from God, so Christianity and the New Age both see the solution as coming back to God. However, Christians believe man is unable to come back to God, because man is corrupted by sin. So God took the initiative and became incarnate; that is, He took upon Himself human flesh in the Person of Jesus Christ: "And the Word became flesh and dwelt among us; and we beheld His glory, the glory as of the only begotten of the Father, full of grace and truth" (John 1:14). As the incarnate Son of God, Jesus Christ died upon the Cross for the sin of the world, thereby paying the penalty for us. But we still could not come back to Him, because the human will is bound in sin. So God the Holy Spirit had to take the initiate once again and through His grace draw us unto himself. Redemption, in the Christian view, is grace, the work of God 100 percent. We receive it in faith, which is itself the gift of God (Eph. 2:8-9).

In the New Age view, the solution is to come back to God. But God is nature, so getting back to God means getting back to nature. And that is primarily man's responsibility, because man is the most highly conscious part of nature. Thus the mantle of leadership in the salvation process must of necessity fall upon man.

So how does man get back to nature? It is toward this end that the New Age movement directs its efforts. And remember, in New Age thought we create our own reality; to each his own truth, and all paths lead to God. In no way do I claim to have listed all New Age methods of getting back to nature, but here are a few of the most common.

## OUTDOOR ACTIVITY

Part of getting back to nature is being in close physical proximity to nature. New Age enthusiasts frequently immerse themselves in such activities as sunbathing and backpacking, nature walks, etc. New Agers seem to frequent places of natural beauty such as Aspen, Colorado, Taos, New Mexico, and Sun Valley, Idaho. Just being in close proximity to nature is thought to enable people to adjust their vibrations to the vibrations of the Earth Mother. Margot Adler says there is "no separation between the spiritual and the earthly; there is no retreat from the world of matter."[2] Many regard city living as unnatural since they are separated from nature by concrete and plastic and since they must transport the necessities of survival from outside the city. Some dislike modern technology, even though they find it necessary to use it. Others, however, have adjusted to urban living and technology and are optimistic about its future uses.[3] Adler describes the common traits of neo-pagans as "that sense of childlike wonder, acceptance of life and death, attunement to the rhythms of nature, sense of humor, lack of guilt-ridden feelings about oneself and about the body and sexuality, genuine honesty, and unwillingness or inability to play social games."[4]

Now, there is nothing wrong with loving nature. Our family lives in the country, and I love being more in touch with nature. I love hiking, backpacking, horseback riding, canoeing, cross-country skiing and the like; one of my favorite activities is just jogging or walking with my dog in the woods by our home.

Christians should appreciate nature. Through nature we see the handiwork of God: His majesty, His power, His glory, His design, His orderliness, His constancy, His infinite variety, But we do not worship nature. We may learn of God through nature, but we do not come back to God through nature.

## NATURAL FOODS

Two types of people seem to be especially interested in natural foods: Evangelical Christians, and New Agers.

Many are very devoted to natural foods, and strongly believe they should stay away from processed foods, artificial chemicals, etc.

That being the case, let me say at the outset that I am a strong believer in natural foods. Marlene and I belong to a natural foods co-op.

We grind our own wheat and bake our own bread (although Marlene might question my use of the word "we"!). We are not fanatical about it; occasionally we go out for pizza and Dr. Pepper, and it's difficult to maintain a good diet while you're on a lecture tour.

But we believe natural foods help to maintain good health.

So I have no objection to natural foods. My concern is that New Agers make a religion out of it.

The New Age emphasizes vegetarianism and natural foods as a means of being closer to nature. They also argue that it is wrong to eat meat, because man is part of nature and when a person eats an animal he is eating a distant relative. Some claim vegetarians are higher on the evolutionary scale than meat-eaters — a claim for which there is no basis whatsoever.

But there is another reason for avoiding meat: Red meat is high in protein, and protein interferes with altered states of consciousness (see below). And since some vegetables are also high in protein, some New Agers go even further and restrict themselves to fruit.[5]

The Bible authorizes us to eat meat. In Genesis 9 God made his covenant with Noah and authorized man to eat meat; this covenant is expressly and repeatedly stated to be a perpetual covenant applying to all generations and indeed even to all flesh. Christ fed loaves and fishes to the five thousand, and He gave His disciples bread and meat at the Last Supper. He would not have done so if eating meat was either sinful or unhealthy.

God's Word permits us to eat meat, but it does not command us to eat meat. If you want to be a vegetarian, that's fine. But don't make a religion out of it; it is not a path to God.

### HARNESSING POWERS OF NATURE

As Jeffrey Burton Russell observes, the distinction between magic and religion is that "magic attempts to control the powers of the Universe; religion supplicates them."[6] In this way magic and science have much in common. Science is much more precise in its identification of the powers of the universe and its methods of harnessing them, for science defines them strictly in secular terms. Magic sees the forces of the universe as both natural and supernatural; in fact, magicians seem to fuse the natural and supernatural as though there were no sharp distinction between them. One, Isaac Bonawitz, has called himself a materialist and adds, "I just define matter a little more loosely."[7] Or as Leo Martello says, "I make no claims as a witch to 'supernatural powers,' but I totally believe in the super powers that reside in the natural."[8] Accordingly, the magician's methods of controlling the forces of nature are going to be looser and less precise.

One means of controlling the forces of nature involves the use of crystals. As you know, a prism concentrates light and diffuses it into the various colors of the rainbow. In the New Age view crystals, because of their prism shape, concentrate and diffuse the forces of nature. New Age thinkers have written numerous books describing the properties of crystals and explaining how to harness the power of crystals to bring oneself success, power, health and happiness by wearing crystals in certain ways and by placing them in various strategic positions around one's body and around one's dwelling.[9]

Another method is astrology. Unlike astronomy which is simply the scientific study of the stars, astrology is the belief that the positions of the stars both control and predict events on earth.

While there are many theories of astrology, the general belief is that events on earth are but a microcosm of events going on across the vast universe. As the famous Satanist Aleister Crowley used to say, "As above, so below."[10]

Many astrologers believe the universe is made up of vibrating energy, or cosmic energy. The Zodiac consists of twelve constellations of stars, each of which is in ascendency in the sky for about one month of the year. Each sign of the Zodiac has its own atmosphere or cosmic energy. When a child takes his first breath right after birth, the atmosphere he draws in gives him his cosmic identity, which of course will depend upon which sign is in the ascendency at the time. Thus a person born under the sign of Libra will have a special identification with the constellation and Zodiac sign of Libra; a person born under Taurus will be identified with the sign of Taurus, etc. Knowing the unique strengths and weaknesses and futures that are likely to befall a person helps a person know what to expect for himself and how to deal with people of various signs. Leading astrologers devote their considerable time and talents toward development of highly imaginative astrological horoscopes.

In my opinion astrology makes no sense whatsoever, either from a scriptural standpoint or from a scientific standpoint. It is sheer nonsense. Nevertheless, the shelves of bookstores are filled with astrology books. Most major newspapers carry astrology columns, and millions of Americans slavishly follow their advice. Why?

For one thing, prophecies often tend to be self-fulfilling. The reader is told, "You will meet a new friend today." So he is extra friendly as he looks for this new friend, and it pays off. Or he is told, "Don't take unnecessary risks today or you could have a serious accident." (Note the subjective words "unnecessary," "could," and "serious." So he stays home all day, and sure enough, he avoids an accident; so he is eternally grateful to the astrologer who warned him of the danger lurking around the corner.

Astrologers usually describe your personality traits in language that can apply to almost anyone. Phrases like "You are normally calm and even-tempered but occasionally you have an angry outburst," or "Your usual happy state of mind can be upset by depression when things really get rough" lead the hopeful reader to think, "That's me all right!"

And astrologers and other occult prophets stress their successes and ignore their failures. An astrologer might predict, "A great leader will die this year." Every year, somewhere in the world, a leader dies; so when a provincial governor in Bolivia passes away, the astrologer claims his prophecy has been fulfilled.

But while astrology has no actual merit, Satan

can use it to cause people to depend on him rather than God. While Satan is not omniscient like God, he is far more intelligent and better informed than we are. While Satan cannot know the future the way God does, his knowledge, intellect and experience enable him to make some shrewd guesses. When these predictions are communicated through demons to the astrologer, and the astrologer uses it to make an accurate prediction, his credibility is enhanced and he is thought to have miraculous powers.

The same could be said of tarot card reading, of Ouija boards, of palm reading, and other means of foretelling the future. Most of it is pure charlatanry. But that which is real is deadly. For demons can work through these means to lead people away from God and into dependence upon Satan instead.

In August 1987, New Agers gathered at the top of Pike's Peak in Colorado and at other locations throughout the world to partake of the "harmonic convergence." This was a unique planetary formation; the planets were aligned in such a way that cosmic energy was heavily concentrated and available for those who knew how to receive it. This, again, was a New Age attempt to get with the forces of nature and harness them for man's use.

Sex and nudity are central themes in some (but not all) New Age practices. Some believe one can give and receive cosmic energy more fully while nude than while clothed. Sexual activity, particularly as part of a ritual, is a means of expressing and partaking in the divine energy of the universe.

Another means of gaining power over the forces of nature is through "magic words," spells or incantations. Certain words are believed to possess special power. When used in a certain way, or in certain combinations, the use of such words can change things. One can use these forces to bring good results for oneself and one's friends; or one can use spells and incantations to cause bad things to happen to one's enemies. Likewise, numbers are thought to have certain power, particularly in certain combinations. The letters that make up words are powerful as well. Particularly, many New Agers believe runes have magical powers. Runes are the ancient alphabet used by the Norse and other northern Europeans about a thousand years ago. New Age books are available today in bookstores which explain the magical powers of runes and how to use them.[11]

Certain shapes are thought to have special power. The swastika is one example; it was used in the Near East thousands of years ago as an occult symbol. The same is true of the "broken cross" or "witch's foot," an ancient occult symbol recently resurrected as the so-called "peace symbol." Another is the Egyptian ankh, a cross with an oval at the top. Still another is the pentagram, a five-pointed star-shaped symbol used more by outright Satanists than by other occult practitioners.

Others use physical objects, often called amulets or talismans. These have no power in and of themselves, but provide a focus for the concentration of one's mental energy. Rabbits' feet, hex dolls, etc.

Alchemy is another means of controlling nature. It is an ancient practice whereby the alchemist could supposedly change one element into another, such as changing iron into gold. Alchemy was once widely accepted as a legitimate art or science, endorsed by the most respected scientists of the time. Today most scientists regard alchemy as silly, and Christians would agree. But if one accepts the New Age idea that the universe is made up of energy and that different elements are simply different masses of energy vibrating at different speeds, and if one agrees with the New Age view that thought is a light form of energy and that form tends to follow thought, then it makes sense to think that by concentrating our heightened mental powers upon changing the form of an object, we can cause the energy that is vibrating at the speed of iron to speed up or slow down its vibrations so that it takes on the form of gold. And this becomes all the more believable if one accepts the New Age view that perception is reality and that it's all in our minds anyway.

The same reasoning applies to "shapeshifting."

Incredible though it may seem to some, many in
the occult today take very seriously the old tales
of vampires, ghouls, werewolves and of witches
turning themselves or others into cats or frogs. In
fact, a recent edition of the *Denver Post* carried an
advertisement for a seminar on shapeshifting led
by a woman who advertises herself as holding a
doctorate of philosophy in education. Again, if all
that we perceive as matter is really just vibrating
energy, and if form tends to follow thought, then
it follows that with the right powers of concentrated thought plus the added power of spells and
incantations one could change one's own shape
into that of another person or an animal, or one
could change another person in the same way. It
is interesting to note that in *Malleus Malificarum*,
the treatise of Heinrich Kramer and James
Sprenger written around 1484 to justify the
Inquisition's role in the suppression of witchcraft,
the authors conclude witches do not have power to
actually change form but do have the power to
create the illusion of change in form. That is, a
witch could not change a person into a cat, but she
could create an illusion whereby a person appears
as a cat to other people.[12]

## ALTERED STATES OF CONSCIOUSNESS

Shamanism has been defined as opening a door
to a different reality. A shaman is one who enters
an altered state of consciousness and goes on a

journey in order to gather knowledge from a different reality. While altered states of consciousness may seem different from harnessing the powers of nature, we must remember once again that in New Age thought perception is reality.

One means of entering an altered state of consciousness is through ritual. Ritual, Margot Adler says, is "one method of reintegrating individuals and groups into the cosmos, and to tie in the activities of daily life with their ever present, often forgotten, significance. It allows us to feel biological connectedness with ancestors who regulated their lives and activities according to seasonal observances."[13] Bonawitz defines ritual as "any ordered sequence of events or actions, including directed thoughts, especially one that is repeated in the 'same' manner each time, and that is designed to produce a predictable altered state of consciousness within which certain magical or religious results may be obtained," with the purpose of putting you into an altered state "within which you have access to and control over your psychic talents."[13] Various pagan groups have rediscovered rituals of the past or recreated new rituals reflecting ancient Celtic, or Teutonic, or Egyptian, or other traditions.

One role of these rituals is to harness the power of the gods. Are the gods real? Remember, perception is reality. Aidan Kelly argues that the

Goddess is real "because human energy goes into making Her real; She exists as a 'thought form on the astral plane,' yet She can manifest physically whenever She wants to. She does not exist independently of mankind, but She is most thoroughly independent of any one person or group."[15] The role of ritual, then, is to concentrate our cosmic energy on the task of making the gods real, or bringing them down to earth. As David Miller says, the task at hand is to incarnate the gods, to "become aware of their presence, acknowledge and celebrate their forms."[16]

"Casting the circle" is a central feature of many pagan rituals. Margot Adler puts it this way:

> Most Wiccans work within a circle, "a portable temple," as one Witch wrote to me. Certain groups in England have been known to set up a psychic "castle," and many Witches will tell you that their circle is really a sphere. The circle is the declaration of sacred ground. It is a place set apart, although its material location may be a living room or a backyard. But in the mind the circle, reinforced by the actions of casting it and purifying it, becomes sacred space, a place "between the worlds" where contact with archetypal reality, within the deep places of the mind — with "gods," if you will — becomes possible. It is a place where time disappears, where history is obliterated. It is the contact point between two realities. ...
>
> Craft ritual usually starts with casting and creating this magical space and ritually purifying it with the ancient elements: fire, water, earth, and air. The circle is cast with a ritual sword, wand, or athame (a small, usually black-handled and double-bladed dag-

ger that is used by almost all covens, whatever their tradition). Different covens have different symbologies, but often the sword represents fire, the wand (or incense burner) air, the cup water, and the pentacle — a round, inscribed disk of wax or metal — earth. When the circle is cast, often the gods and goddesses are invoked.

Some covens use music, chanting, and dancing to raise psychic energy within the circle. Psychic healing is often attempted, with varying degrees of success. The most common form of "working" is known as "raising a cone of power." This is done by chanting or dancing (or both) or running around the circle. The "cone of power" is really the combined wills of the group, intensified through ritual and meditative techniques, focused on an end collectively agreed upon. Usually a priestess or priest directs the cone; when she or he senses that it has been raised, it is focused and directed with the mind and shot toward its destination.

Many covens also engage in more "spiritual" or "religious" workings. Many of the revivalist covens have rituals in which the Goddess, symbolized by the moon, is "drawn down" into a priestess of the coven who, at times, goes into trance and is "possessed by" or "incarnates" the Goddess force. Similarly, there are rituals where the God force is drawn down into the priest who takes the role of the God in the circle. In these rituals Witches become the gods within the circle, actualizing that potentiality. When done well, these can be among the most powerful experiences. I have seen people really change in such rituals. I have also seen these rituals become shams.[17]

Adler explains further that "The circle is the microcosm of the universe, a place apart from the world and protected. It is a positive environment in which the serpents of one's own psyche can reveal themselves creatively."[18] She also notes that these rituals commonly take place on the "sabbats," the great festivals of European Paganism. The major sabbats are "Samhain (Halloween or November Eve); the Celtic New Year, the day when the walls between the worlds were said to be thinnest and when contact with one's ancestors took place; Oimelc (February 1), the winter purification festival, the time of the beginning of spring movement; Beltane (May 1), the great fertility festival, the marriage of God and Goddess; Lughnasadh (August 1), the festival of first fruits and, in some traditions, the time of the fight between the bull and stag god for the Lady, or the death of the Sacred King."[19] Other common times for rituals are the summer and winter solstices and fall and spring equinoxes, and full moons or new moons. Adler says, "These festivals renew a sense of living communion with natural cycles, with the changes of season and land."[20]

The marriage of the God and Goddess is used in some but not all covens. According to Adler, " ... in its highest form, the 'Great Rite,' often alluded to by the media, is a sublime religious experience. Properly understood, it is not — as the press would have us believe — the carryings on of bored suburban swingers. The idea behind the 'Great Rite' is that a woman who, through ritual, has 'incarnated' or become the Goddess, and a man who, through ritual, has 'incarnated' or become

the God — in other words, two people who have
drawn down into themselves these archetypal
forces, or, if you will, have allowed these forces
within them to surface — can have a spiritual and
physical union that is truly divine."[21]

The many occult rituals involve infinite variety.
Many traditions have sprung up over the years in
different parts of the world, and some modern
occultists have tried to pattern themselves after
an ancient tradition that intrigues them, such as
that of the Celts, or the Teutons, or the Norse, or
the Greeks, or the Egyptians. Sometimes they
have discovered ancient traditions and adapted
them for modern use; sometimes they recreate
these old traditions.

There is some debate as to whether these groups
reflect a continuous tradition from ancient to
modern times. But in the New Age view, perception is reality. So it matters not whether the
tradition is continuous or not. What matters is
whether you believe in it now, and whether it
works for you.

## VISUALIZATION

Other New Agers use less dramatic means of
harnessing cosmic energy within their minds.
Shakti Gawain urges her readers to use "creative
visualization to "create a sanctuary within yourself
where you can go anytime you want to. Your
sanctuary is your ideal place of relaxation, tran-

quility and safety and you can create it exactly as you want it."

She then describes a process by which the reader can visualize an ideal place such as "in a meadow, on a mountaintop, in the forest, beside the sea. It could even be under the ocean, or on another planet." She urges the reader to explore his new sanctuary, making any improvements or changes he desires, and then says, "From now on this is your own personal inner sanctuary, to which you can return at any time just by closing your eyes and desiring to be there. You will always find it healing and relaxing to be there. It is also a place of special power for you, and you may wish to go there every time you do creative visualization."[22]

This personal sanctuary is much like the circle cast by the pagan priestess, a place created by or in the mind that is specially reserved for your own private version of reality.

After you have entered this private sanctuary, this inner circle or microcosm of your own universe, you are likely to find that you are not alone: You will be joined by your "spirit guide."

As Shakti Gawain says, "Each one of us has all the wisdom and knowledge we ever need right within us. It is available to us through our intuitive mind, which is our connection with universal intelligence. However, we often find it difficult to connect with our higher wisdom. One of the best ways to do so is by meeting and getting to know our inner guide."[23]

Who is this spirit guide? As Ms. Gawain says, "The inner guide is known by many different names, such as your counselor, spirit guide, imaginary friend, or master. It is a higher part of yourself, which can come to you in many different forms, but usually comes in the form of a person or being whom you can talk to and relate to as a wise and loving friend."[24]

Many New Agers would not agree that the spirit guide is simply a higher part of oneself. Some would say their spirit guides are gods, or angelic beings. More would say their spirit guides are spirits of departed persons who have gained great wisdom in their previous lives and are generously willing to impart this wisdom to those of us who are not so far advanced on the evolutionary scale of consciousness.

Others have given various names to their spirit guides. Some claim allegiance for a very wise and powerful spirit guide whom they call "Lord Mantreya." Other New Age persons who have adopted Christianity as their personal path to truth, believe Jesus or Mary is their spirit guide. Others might believe their spirit guide to be Buddha, or Confucious, or Nefertiti, or another wise person of antiquity. For others, their spirit guide might be a departed ancestor.

Shakti Gawain suggests an exercise by which

you can go to your private sanctuary and meet your spirit guide. (The exercise will not be quoted or described here because I do not want to lead anyone into experimentation with the occult.) She says,

> Now show your guide around your sanctuary and explore it together. Your guide may point out some things that you've never seen there before, or you may enjoy just being in each other's presence.
>
> Ask your guide if there is anything he or she would like to say to you, or any advice to give you at the moment. If you wish, you can ask some specific questions. You may get immediate answers, but if not, don't be discouraged, the answers will come to you in some form later.
>
> When the experience of being together feels complete for now, thank your guide and express your appreciation, and ask him or her to come to meet you in your sanctuary again.[25]

## CHANNELING

Spirit guides provide good advice, good company, good affirmation and moral support, but some do even more. Some even write books!

The New Age movement uses many books that claim to be "channelled writings." The spirit guide, desiring to impart his wisdom to the entire human race, takes control of one's mind and writes a book, using your mind and your fingers as a channel. The effort is yours, and the book may come out in your name. You may even get the royalties! But the ideas in the book are those of the spirit guide who used you as his channel to get the book before the human race.

Does this really happen? I don't know, but many New Agers believe it does. I have read several books that purport to be channelled writings. For example is *Exploring Atlantis*, the human author of which is Dr. Frank Alper. The back cover describes Dr. Alper as

> ...a well known and respected teacher of metaphysics and spiritual growth throughout the country. He founded the Arizona Metaphysical Society in 1974. Having completed his initiations in 1985, he was given the spiritual name of "Christos," which means "The Enlightened One." Since that time he has become one with his soul "Adamis," and channels his truth at a concious [sic] level.[26]

But Dr. Alper is only the human author. Another being has channelled his truth through Dr. Alper's body and mind. This spirit guide begins Chapter One with the salutation,

> We speak to you tonight as Atemose II, Ruler of Atlantis. Blessings to you.[27]

Atmose II proceeds to relate to us how Atlantis was destroyed, and how Atlantis was home to many people, some good and some evil. But God gave the Elders of Atlantis a special mission: to resettle the earth and recreate the world's civilizations. Atmose then speaks of the Garden of Eden and the "symbolic Adam and Eve and the snake."[28] Abraham, Isaac, and Jacob all were Ascended Masters, formerly of Atlantis.

Atmose then informs us that "Jacob and his wife bore unto themselves twelve sons,"[29] apparently forgetting that Jacob had *two* wives, Rachel and Leah, plus two concubines. Leah bore six sons and Rachel bore two while the concubines Zilpah and Bilhah bore the others. (Is it possible that a spirit guide would not know that?)

Then Atmose tells us of Jesus Christ — or his version of Jesus Christ:

> There came a point in the evolution of your history when an Emissary from God incarnated upon the surface of Earth. The Elders were informed of the impending presence of this soul, and they gathered together. When the Soul assumed the place in the physical child, ancient vibrations and reactions rose to the surface. Jealousies manifested themselves. The Elders of Atlantis denied the presence of the Master Jesus within the physical body....
>
> Why did that Master Soul come into physical form? What was the function for these vibrations? ...A force of unity, an expression of power, had been determined to be necessary to walk among mankind. This was done to reunite the bonds of man and God....
>
> What happened to those Elders of Atlantis who called themselves Hebrews when they denied God? Some historians say that, from that time, the race of Hebrews have suffered and lived as nomads; that they have wandered and been denied their homeland; that they have been persecuted throughout the world; that as a race of people they have been born to suffer, to cleanse themselves of sin. This is, of course, invalid, for there is no sin.

> You who are sitting and reading these words are part of these vibrations of rejection. For many, it is part of the reason that you are here now at this time, to learn that there never was a necessity to carry the guilt; that there never was a necessity to punish because of rejection; that it was only the decision of the conscious mind, of the generations of vibrations of guilt that man imposed upon itself.[30]

I seriously doubt that a spirit guide wrote this book, because, quite frankly, I don't think a good self-respecting spirit guide would put his imprimatur on something that stupid! At least a spirit guide would avoid spelling and grammar errors and would get his facts of history correct! (Question: Would a spirit guide have standing to sue me for libel?) Nevertheless, I do not rule out the possibility that supernatural powers could use human agencies to write books.

Shakti Gawain is very uncritical in her acceptance of her spirit guide. She says, "Basically if you feel good about your experience, then it's fine. If not, be creative and do whatever you need to do to change it."[31]

But there are dangers here. Retreating to this "private sanctuary" can become a habit, a cop-out, a retreat from having to face reality act upon it. It could lead to withdrawal and possibly even to autism, though admittedly its stated purpose is the opposite.

The uncritical acceptance of this so-called spirit guide is very dangerous. Shakti Gawain just says, if you feel good about it, it's fine. But Scripture says, "There is a way that seemeth right unto a man, but the ends thereof are the way of death" (Prov. 14:12; 16:25). Since the human heart and mind can err, Scripture exhorts us to "test the spirits, to see whether they are of God" (1 John 4:1).

Much, perhaps most, of what people call spirit guides or channelled writings are mere fantasy and self-delusion, like the imaginary playmate many of us daydreamed about as children. But the creation of an imaginary spirit guide in your mind is an easy avenue for demon possession. It is an easy way for demons to enter your mind undetected, set up residence there, and control your mind and your life.

At first it may seem all sweetness and light. Like the spirit guide described by Shakti Gawain, the demon may appear to be kind, wise, helpful, generous and loving. Scripture warns us that "Satan is transformed into an angel of light; so is it not surprising that his ministers should transform themselves into angels of light?" (2 Cor. 11:14-15). But gradually, as the demon is fully in control, his true nature comes out, and the results are fearsome indeed.

There are other means of entering into altered states of consciousness. Transcendental Meditation (TM) is one such method. A form of yoga, TM has its roots in Hindu religion. It is based upon the Hindu belief that every human being consists of prakrti and purusha. Prakrti consists of a person's body, mind, and conscious self or ego. Purusha is pure, empty consciousness, or, in Hindu thought, the soul. While there are many varieties of yoga, generally they consist of various stages of exercise and concentration in which the person develops that state of concentration in which he can realize that his soul is pure and free, empty of all content. Having reached that stage, he can gain moksha, or release from the cycle of rebirth and reincarnation in which Hindus believe.[32]

Some karate and other Oriental self-defense techniques utilize yoga, TM, or other similar practices as part of the conditioning for learning the sport. I am not saying you and your children should not take karate lessons, but I am saying you should check it out carefully before you do. And a simple denial that TM or yoga is being taught may not be sufficient. All too often these techniques are introduced under a different name, or with no name at all, simply as relaxation techniques, or as meditation, or as mind control or mind expansion, or as training in creative thinking.

Drugs are another means of entering altered states of consciousness. So is illicit sex. So is music. New Age music is difficult to define, and not everything that is placed on the New Age shelf in the music store fits that category. One music store clerk related to a friend of mine that they often place records or cassettes under the New Age heading because they sell better there, or because they don't know where else to put them. It can probably best be defined as "mellow" music that causes you to relax, let your guard down, and uncritically accept whatever enters your eyes and ears. The dangers inherent in such music should be obvious, because it can open your mind and soul to false and dangerous ideas and practices.

Almost any practice that causes wide emotional swings and mesmerizes the individual into the group, can be a path to altered states of consciousness. The danger is that when you enter these altered states, you are no longer in conscious control of your mind. The helm of your mind is left unattended, and another being, perhaps a demon, can take control instead.

While I was stationed with the Air Force at Grand Forks Air Force Base, North Dakota, I became acquainted with a man who had been involved in witchcraft, but had broken from it completely and had become a Christian. He testimony is a great blessing to all. He explains that Satan deceived him by approaching him at his point of need. As a teenager, he says, he was kind of a wallflower, not particularly handsome, athletic or popular. But through witchcraft he learned to become the center of attention. At dances and parties he could play mind tricks on others and quickly become the life of the party.

"I didn't know Satan was behind it," he says." I just thought I was using the powers of nature. That's the way it starts. But it doesn't stay that way. Gradually, as you become more involved, the tables are turned. Before you even realize it, you are no longer using the powers; the powers are using you."

Satan is not tame or docile. Scripture says he is a roaring lion, seeking whom he may devour.(1 Pet. 5:8). He will appear as a docile creature, as a humble servant, as an angel of light. But he won't stay that way for long. Soon he will control you and use you as a tool for his purposes. And when he is through using you, he will destroy you.

## CANAAN — THE ORIGINAL NEW AGERS

That is why God commanded the Hebrews to have nothing to do with the occult. The Canaanites who had occupied Palestine before Joshua and the Hebrews conquered it, engaged in Baal-worship, fertility rites, child sacrifice, and temple prostitution; and for this reason, God enabled the Hebrews to conquer the land and take it from them. And God spoke through Moses and declared to the Hebrews,

> When thou art come into the land which the Lord thy God giveth thee, thou shalt not learn to do after the abominations of those nations. There shall not be found among you any one that maketh his son or his

daughter to pass through the fire, or that useth divination, or an observer of times, or an enchanter, or a
witch, or a charmer, or a consulter with familiar
spirits, or a wizard, or a necromancer. For all that do
these things are an abomination unto the Lord: and
because of these abominations the Lord thy God doth
drive them out from before thee. Thou shalt be perfect
before the Lord thy God. For these nations, which thou
shalt possess, hearkened unto observers of times, and
unto diviners: but as for thee, the Lord thy God hat not
suffered thee so to do (Deut. 18:9-14).

How, then can we come to God? How do we find
salvation? How do we know spiritual truth? God
answers that question in the next verse:

> The Lord thy God will raise up unto thee a Prophet
> from the midst of thee, of thy brethren, like unto me;
> unto him ye shall hearken (Deut. 18:15).

We come to God through His Son, the Lord
Jesus Christ, who died on a cross for our sins, and
who gave us His revealed Word, the Bible, as our
source of truth. We find salvation and truth by
turning to Jesus Christ and His Word, not the
false prophets of the New Age.

## ENDNOTES

1. Shakti Gawain, *Creative Visualization* (San
Rafale, California: New World Library, 1978), p.
64.

2. Margot Adler, *Drawing Down the Moon*
(Boston: Beacon Press, 1979, 1986), p. 372.

3. Ibid., pp. 376-398.

4. Adler, p. 383.

5. Dr. Rebecca Brown, M.D., *He Came To Set the Captives Free* (Chino, California: Chick Publications, 1986), pp. 184-185.

6. Jefferey Burton Russell, *Witchcraft In the Middle Ages* (Ithaca, New York: Cornell University Press, 1972), p.10.

7. Isaac Bonewits, quoted by Adler, p. 397.

8. Leo Martello, *Witchcraft: The Old Religion* (Secaucus, New Jersey: University Books, 1973), p.12; quote by Adler, p. 154.

9. Ra Bonewitz, *Cosmic Crystals: Crystal Consciousness and the New Age* (Wellingborough, Northhamptonshire, England: Aquarian Pres, 1983, 1987), generally.

10. Aleister Crowley, *Magick In Theory and Practice* (New York: Castle, n.d.), p. 11; quoted by Gary North, *Unholy Spirits* (Fort Worth, Texas: Dominion Press, 1986), p. 335.

11. Donald Tyson, *Rune Magic* (St. Paul, Minnesota: Llewellyn Publications, 1988), generally.

12. Heinrich Kramer and James Sprenger, *Malleus Maleficarum*, circa 1484 (reprinted by Dover Publications of New York, 1971), translated by Rev. Montague Summers, Part One, Question X, pp. 61-65.

13. Adler, p. 162.

14. Bonewits, quoted by Adler, p. 161.

15. Aidan Kelly, quoted by Adler, p. 172.

16. David Miller, *The New Polytheism* (New York:

Harper & Row, 1974), p. 81; quoted by Adler, p. 31).

17. Adler, pp. 109-110
18. Ibid., p.1.
19. Gawain, pp. 89-90
20. Ibid., p. 159.
21. Ibid., pp. 110-111
22. Ibid., p. 111
23. Ibid., P. 110
24. Ibid., p. 91
25. Ibid.
26. Ibid., p. 92.
27. Dr. Frank Alper, *Exploring Atlantis, Vol. III* (Irvine, California: Quantum Productions, 1986), back cover.
28. Ibid., p. 4.
29. Ibid., p. 4.
30. Ibid., pp. 5-6.
31. Gawain, p. 92.
32. *The World Book Encyclopedia*, 1985, s.v. "Yoga."

*CHAPTER NINE*

# BATTLING THE NEW AGE

"For we wrestle not against flesh and blood, but against principalities, against powers, against the rulers of darkness of this world, against spiritual wickedness in high places" (Eph. 6:12).

As the twenty-first century approaches, Christianity finds itself locked in a struggle for its very existence. Its opponent, the New Age movement, is as dangerous as any other system Satan has raised to date. It is subtle, deceptive, fascinating, beautiful, and captivating. Denying absolute truth, the New Age movement disguises itself in whatever mode appears most attractive at the time. In this way Satan meets each person at his or her point of greatest weakness.

Let us then carefully consider how to do battle against this most formidable foe.

(1) Be aware of Satan and his devices.

I remind you once again of the admonition of C.S. Lewis: "There are two equal and opposite errors into which our race can fall about the devils. One is to disbelieve in their existence. The other is to believe, and to feel an excessive and unhealthy interest in them. They themselves are equally pleased by both errors, and hail a materialist or a magician with the same delight."[1]

Disbelief in, or ignorance of, Satan and his demons is dangerous. If we are ignorant about Satan and demons, we are likely to be deceived by them. It is said that Martin Luther once became so conscious of the presence of Satan in his study that he picked up his inkwell and hurled it at the Devil — not that Satan is deathly afraid of inkwells, but certainly Luther through this symbolic gesture affirmed his determination to stand with God and against the Devil. Luther's great hymn *A Mighty Fortress* shows his consciousness of the presence of Satan in our world:

> ...For still our ancient foe
> Doeth seek to work us woe;
> His craft and power are great,
> And, armed with cruel hate,
> On earth is not his equal.

Like Luther, we need to be conscious of Satan's working in our world, and we need to be educated, through Scripture and through good Christian materials, as to how Satan works. If we are ignorant of Satan, we are likely to be deceived by Satan.

(2) Don't get "hooked" on the New Age.

The other danger C.S. Lewis warned about — a danger less common today, but more deadly for those it afflicts — is developing an unhealthy interest in Satanism. Like the vice officer who becomes entrapped in the very vices he is battling, the Christian who devotes himself to fighting and exposing the New Age can find himself attracted to, and ultimately captured by, the very enemy he is fighting.

There is something in the soul of man that is attracted to and fascinated by the occult. The New Age message, with its emphasis on peace and love, oneness with nature, mellowness, good vibrations, the God within, etc., is very appealing. The thought that one can harness the forces of nature, or make much greater use of one's own brainpower and creativity, sounds very tempting to one who can't seem to find the time and energy to get everything done right now. Little by little, as one becomes exposed to New Age ideas and practices, they become less and less offensive, more and more tolerable, and eventually, more and more tempting. Gradually one becomes enmeshed in their spell.

It's easy to rationalize one's involvement with the occult. "I'm a Christian; this stuff can't hurt me." or, "I'm not really interested in this stuff; I'm just reading it (or watching it, or doing it) so I can be better informed."

*Christian: Yes, the occult can hurt you!* As Peter reminds us, "Your adversary, the devil, as a roaring lion, walketh about, seeking whom he may devour"

(1 Pet. 5:8). He is the great deceiver, who trans-
forms himself into an angel of light (2 Cor. 11:14-15).
He doesn't appear as a repulsive ogre; rather, he
appears to each of us in whatever disguise is most
attractive to us — and remember, sin is not really
a temptation unless it is first made attractive!

Consequently, I do not recommend that every
Christian become an expert on the New Age
movement or the occult. New Age material is
readily available on the shelves of most bookstores
and public libraries. Much of it is intensely
practical (if the New Age can be called practical in
any sense), with easy and simple one-two-three
steps to learn to enter an altered state of consciousness, project your astral body, etc. This is
dangerous material! Even though it may not
tempt you now, if you have that information in
your mind you may be tempted to try it in a
moment of weakness sometime in the future.

I therefore strongly urge Christian readers to
stay away from New Age materials unless God
has placed a special calling upon you to research
this subject — and even then, do so carefully and
with prayer. There are plenty of good writings on
the New Age movement, written from a distinctively Christian standpoint, that will give you all
the information you need. For those who feel they
must read the New Agers' own works, I suggest
Margot Adler's *Drawing Down the Moon* (Boston:
Beacon Press, 1979, 1986) as a perceptive, factual,

even-handed and well-rounded coverage of the movement in general.

Somewhere between these two extremes — disbelief in or ignorance of Satan, and an unhealthy interest in Satanism — is the wisest course for the Christian to follow.

(3) Stand in God's strength.

Do not think yourself strong enough, or wise enough, or virtuous enough, to stand against Satan in your own power. You aren't, and you can't! Luther recognized this in the second stanza of that great hymn:

> Did we in our own strength confide
>  Our striving would be losing;
> Were not the right Man on our side,
>  The Man of God's own choosing.
> Dost ask who that may be?
>  Christ Jesus, it is he;
> Lord Sabaoth his Name,
>  From age to age the same,
> And he must win the battle.

Satan and his demons are stronger, smarter, and more capable than we are. But they are still finite creatures. They are not omnipotent, omniscient, or omnipresent as God is. Their power is greater than ours, but nothing comparable to that of God. That's why we read in the Book of Jude that even Michael the archangel, commander of the angelic armies, when disputing with Satan over the body of Moses (a probable reference to an extracanonical work called "The Assumption of Moses"), did not rebuke Satan in his own strength, but rather invoked the power of God, saying "The Lord rebuke thee" (Jude 9).

Paul therefore tells us:

> Put on the whole armour of God, that ye may be able to stand against the wiles of the devil. For we wrestle not against flesh and blood, but against principalities, against powers, against the rulers of darkness of this world, against spiritual wickedness in high places. Wherefore take unto you the whole armour of God, that ye may be able to withstand in the evil day, and having done all, to stand. Stand therefore, having your loins girt about with truth, and having on the breast-plate of righteousness; And your feet shod with the preparation of the gospel of peace; Above all, taking the shield of faith, wherewith ye shall be able to quench all the fiery darts of the wicked. And take the helmet of salvation, and the sword of the Spirit, which is the word of God (Eph. 6:13-17).

This is more than just adopting a holy posture or using magic words like "The Lord rebuke thee" as an amulet or charm against evil. It is a firm reliance upon the strength found in God and His Word. It includes trusting Jesus Christ and His Death on the Cross as the full remission for our sins. It includes study of the Word of God, so that one may think from God's standpoint and partake of the wisdom God shares with us. It includes the development of strong Christian character, for Satan is ingenious at knowing our moral weaknesses and exploiting them as chinks in our armor.

It includes regular confession of sin, so that no unconfessed sin interferes with our fellowship with God. It means a life totally given over to God, so that God the Holy Spirit fills us and empowers us. And it leads, not to passivity, but to wise and resolute action, empowered by God and ordered by His Word.

For it is ultimately the Word of God that will defeat Satan. God's Word is closely identified with His Son Jesus Christ: "And the Word was made flesh and dwelt among us..." (John 1:14; cf Rev. 19). That's why Luther could say, in the third stanza of his triumphant hymn:

> And though this world, with devils filled,
>   Should threaten to undo us;
> We will not fear, for God hath willed
>   His truth to triumph through us.
> The prince of darkness grim,
>   We tremble not for him;
> His rage we can endure,
>   For lo! his doom is sure,
> One little word shall fell him.

(4) Know what your children are learning!

Humanists and New Agers alike see the minds of our youth as the major battleground — and they have no compunction about using *your* tax dollars to turn *your* children against *your* beliefs. John Dunphy recently declared in *The Humanist* magazine:

> I am convinced that the battle for humankind's

future must be waged and won in the public school classroom by teachers who correctly perceive their role as the proselytizers of a new faith: a religion of humanity that recognizes and respects the spark of what theologians call divinity in every human being. These teachers must embody the same selfless dedication as the most rabid fundamentalist preacher, for they will be ministers of another servant, utilizing a classroom instead of a pulpit to convey humanist values in whatever subjects they teach regardless of the educational level — preschool daycare or large state university. The classroom must and will become an arena of conflict between the old and the new — the rotting corpse of Christianity, together with all its adjacent evils and misery, and the new faith of humanism resplendent in its promise of a world in which the never realized Christian ideal of "love thy neighbor" will finally be achieved.[2]

There you have it. The enemy has not only publicly declared war; he has even delineated the battlefield. And your children are the prize!

It is vitally important that you know what your children are thinking and learning. You need to maintain good channels of communication with your children, so they will share these things with you. You may also wish to examine the texts they're learning out of, and teachers' manuals as well. Mel and Norma Gabler of Educational Research Analysts, P.O. Box 7518, Longview, Texas 75607, are an excellent source of information on textbooks.

New Age ideas can be taught as part of almost any subject, but some of those to especially watch for are death education, values clarification, health, home economics, sociology, literature, and psychology. Note that I did not say you shouldn't let your child take those courses; I am simply saying that these are some of the subjects in which New Age ideas are most likely to abound.

School is not the only source of New Age ideas, of course. Your child is also influenced by what he reads, what he listens to, what he watches on television and in the movies. Many times we are more susceptible to suggestion while we are being entertained than while we are engaged in serious study.

I'm not going to lay out any hard and fast guidelines as to what your child should and should not watch. Is it dangerous to have your child watch a movie that projects wrong ideas? That depends upon the child, and it also depends upon how you handle it.

Several years ago, when our son David was about twelve, he wanted to see a science fiction movie that his friends were seeing, and Marlene and I were undecided whether to let him or not. Finally I said, "OK, David, you can see the movie; but when you get back I want you to write a 100-word theme telling me what was good about the movie and what was bad about it." The next day he handed me a theme that did an excellent job of pointing out the New Age aspects of the movie. Watching the movie critically in this way probably strengthened David spiritually, for it helped him to identify false ideas in the world. Another idea is to watch the movie with your children, and then discuss it afterwards.

I'm certainly not going to suggest that you do this with every film. I'm not going to send David to an x-rated movie and have him write a theme telling me what was wrong with it! Nor am I going to recommend a steady diet of objectionable programs or movies. Even when viewing these things critically, you can build up a tolerance for them, and eventually even a thirst for them. That's why Paul admonishes,

> Finally, brethren, whatsoever things are true, whatsoever things are honest, whatsoever things are just, whatsoever things are pure, whatsoever things are lovely, whatsoever things are of good report, if there be any virtue, and if there be any praise, think on these things (Phil. 4:8).

(5) Don't jump to conclusions.

Throughout this book we've explained the basic principles of New Age thought and how it is practiced. Lest anyone be falsely accused, we need to throw in a word of caution here: Don't assume that someone is a dedicated New Ager just because he uses a New Age phrase or expresses approval of a New Age idea.

Recently I attended a conference at which one of the speakers, a devout Christian lady, trying to motivate her audience, referred to "cosmic energy." For this, one of her listeners called her a "closet New Ager."

Now, if you've followed the progression of thought in the earlier chapters of this book, you know that "cosmic energy" is a New Age concept. The universe is composed, not of matter, but of energy; and this energy appears as different kinds of matter because it is vibrating at different speeds. People are just complex bundles of energy, and in turn we are all part of one great energy field which we may call Nature or the Earth Mother or God.

But did this Christian lady know that? I am certain that she did not! It was simply a popular and catchy phrase she had picked up somewhere and used without thinking.

Rather than calling her a New Ager, her critic should have approached her discreetly afterward and asked politely, "I noted during your speech that you used the phrase 'cosmic energy.' I'm curious; could you tell me what you mean by that?" This opens the door to explaining, tactfully, how the New Age movement uses the phrase, and you may then be fairly certain that the speaker will scrupulously avoid using the term again.

Likewise, a person may be attracted to one or more of the tenets of New Age thought without buying the whole package or considering himself a New Ager. A Christian who loves the outdoors may find the New Age concept of oneness with nature very attractive, without realizing the implications that are contrary to Christian thought. A person who is concerned about world peace may find globalism an attractive idea until he comes to understand the dangers of world government. A young man who wants to succeed in his profession may be very impressed with courses and programs which promise to expand his mind and enhance his creativity through positive thinking. This does not necessarily mean he has bought the whole New Age package or consciously subscribes to every tenet of New Age thought.

At the same time, a person might hold essentially to a New Age mentality even though he does not agree with every single tenet. I recently had a long and fascinating conversation with a young woman who called herself a witch, who accepts every tenet of New Age thought listed in Chapter 1-7, except one — while she believes God is in nature, she believes He is transcendent (above nature) as well. You might make some tactful inquiries before drawing conclusions.

(6) Attack the idea, not the person.

The New Age is of Satan. It is his lie, possibly the most cunning lie he has devised to date, to deceive and ensnare the human race.

But this does not mean every person who subscribes to New Age thought is a conscious, dedicated servant of Satan. Many claim they do not even believe in Satan — and in most cases I think they sincerely mean it.

Do not make the mistake of assuming that everyone in the New Age movement practices human sacrifice, dances naked in a circle before the full moon, or celebrates the Black Mass on a satanic altar every Halloween night. These overtly Satanic rituals do exist, and they are going on today — and there are recent indications that human sacrifice and the "black arts" are much more widespread than was previously thought, and are increasing rapidly.[3] But they represent only one facet of New Age thought.

Satanists hold to the basic beliefs set forth in Chapters 1-7 of this book, so they must be counted as the "black sheep" of the New Age family. But many in the New Age would like to disown them. One of the best-known New Age cults, that of Wicca, emphasizes that Wicca witches use the powers of nature only for good. The creed of the School of Wicca says in part, "An it harm none, do as you will."[4] (Adler, p. 128) They stand totally opposed to such Satanic practices as human sacrifices, hexes, curses, etc..

"All have sinned and come short of the glory of God," the apostle Paul tells us. (Romans 6:23) New Agers have the same sinful nature as the rest of us, but no worse. In fact, some of the very qualities that cause people to be attracted to the New Age — idealism, gentleness, love of beauty, love of nature, desire for success, desire to find life's meaning — are qualities most of us find admirable.

We will not win these people's hearts for the Lord by lambasting them as Satanists. Rather, we need to show them that the forces they are playing with are dangerous and deadly, and that the answers they so earnestly seek are to be found only in Jesus Christ and His Word.

(7) Take action.

Nevertheless, we need to take firm action when we find that our children are being indoctrinated with New Age concepts or that our tax dollars are being used to promote New Age thought.

If the problem is in a classroom, your first step should be to talk to the teacher. Make sure of your facts before you talk to him, but make clear that your complaint is directed not toward him, but toward what is being taught. He may not even be aware of the New Age implications of his curriculum. If the objection is directed toward a textbook, be prepared to suggest alternative texts if possible. He may agree to stop using the objectionable material, or present it merely as one of several possible ideas, or he may agree to make a special exception for your child.

If this doesn't resolve the problem, you may have to go up the chain of command — to the principal, superintendent, or school board. If the school board members are unsympathetic to your position, you may want to work for the election of someone who shares your views — or run yourself!

(9) Defend your rights in court.

In my books *Christianity and the Constitution* and *The Christian Legal Advisor* (both by Baker Book House of Grand Rapids, Michigan) I demonstrate the Christian foundations of this nation and the drive for religious liberty, primarily by Christians, that led to the adoption of the First Amendment:

> Congress shall make no law respecting an establishment of religion, or prohibiting the free exercise thereof....

The evidence from that period of time points inescapably to the conclusion that the Founders intended the First Amendment to prohibit the federal recognition of one Christian denomination above others as the official religion of the new national government. It seems very unlikely that the Founding Fathers intended the First Amendment to protect Satanism or the occult; certainly their Puritan forebears did not!

Nevertheless, the courts have given the First Amendment an expansive interpretation over the years, interpreting it to include even religions that do not believe in God, such as Secular Humanism (*Torcaso* vs. *Watkins*, 367 U.S. 488, 1961). That being the case, it seems virtually certain that the courts today would recognize New Age and occult religions as covered by the First Amendment today. See, for example, *Ravenwood Church of Wicca* vs. *Roberts*, 292 S.E.2d 657 (1982).

Over the past three decades, the U.S. Supreme Court has interpreted the establishment clause of the First Amendment as prohibiting various Christian practices in the public schools. For example, the Court has prohibited organized prayer led by teachers at the opening of each class period, the reading of the Bible as a daily classroom devotional exercise, and the posting of the Ten Commandments in a public school building.

In *Lemon* vs. *Kurtzman*, 403 U.S. 602 (1971), the Supreme Court ruled that whenever government is involved with religion, three questions must be asked.

These questions, commonly called the "Lemon test," are as follows: (1) Does the governmental activity have a legitimate secular purpose? (2) Does this activity, as its primary effect, advance or inhibit religion? (3) Does this activity involve excessive entanglement of government with religion? A negative answer to any one of these three questions will result in the activity being ruled unconstitutional as an establishment of religion.

Now, let's try an exercise in simple logic:

Major premise:    The First Amendment forbids the establish-

| | |
|---|---|
| | ment of religion. |
| Minor premise: | The New Age is a religion. |
| Conclusion: | The First Amendment forbids the establishment of the New Age. |

To be more precise, courts should examine school curricula and activities to determine and excise New Age content, with the same rigorous scrutiny they use to determine and excise Christian content. But they are not likely to do so unless Christians force the issue by taking schools to court.

A double standard currently exists. Traditional, theistic religions like Christianity, Orthodox Judaism, and Islam are very much restricted in the public arena; but naturalistic religions like the New Age movement, witchcraft, Hinduism, paganism, and the occult are given much more freedom.

For example, many public schools which would prohibit the display of the Christian Cross or the empty tomb at Easter, would allow and encourage Easter eggs and Easter bunnies — yet these are pagan fertility symbols. Others that would prohibit angels and manger scenes at Christmas, encourage witches and goblins at Halloween. Christians need to insist that courts apply the same rigorous establishment clause standard to the New Age movement that they apply to Christianity.

To do so, Christians will need to do their homework. They will have to carefully document what is being taught or promoted, and carefully demonstrate that these are in fact teachings of the New Age movement. They will then have to show a connection between the New Age movement and the concepts being taught in the classroom. As the courts have held in *Harris* vs. *McRae*, (448 U.S. 297, 1980), and *Crowley* vs. *Smithsonian Institution*, (636 F.2d 738, D.C. Cir. 1980), the mere fact that the teachings happen to coincide with the tenets of a religion is probably not sufficient to invoke the establishment clause.

Christians have scored at least one major victory in this regard. New Jersey Christians objected to the teaching of Transcendental Meditation (TM) in the public schools, because TM is a practice of Oriental religions. The schools defended on the ground that TM is just an exercise. The Christians carefully did their homework, proving that TM is being taught in the schools and that TM is in fact a religious practice, clearly related to Eastern religions, and the court agreed. The federal district court banned the teaching of TM in the public schools, and the Circuit Court of Appeals agreed. *Malnak* vs. *Maharishi Mahesh Yogi*, (440 F.Supp. 1284 [1977], affirmed 582 F.2d 197 [1979]).

One would think this would keep TM out of the schools, but it hasn't. TM is in many schools under different names, like synergy, consciousness-raising, or enhanced creativity. I frequently hear of New Age practices in public schools which clearly violate the establishment clause and should be barred if Christians will simply act.

(9) Resist New Age pressures on the job.

All across the country, businesses and governmental offices are being bombarded with New Age thought. "Mr. Businessman, think how your profits would be enhanced if each of your employees could increase his productivity by 50 percent!" And so, businesses pay thousands of dollars to send their employees to seminars where they are taught visualization, positive thinking, and other New Age techniques. The coffers of the New Age movement are enriched, and thousands of business executives and government workers are taught New Age ideas.

If you, as a business executive and a Christian, are required to attend one of these seminars, do you have to do it or lose your job? Probably not, if you can demonstrate that attendance at the seminar would violate your religious convictions.

The Civil Rights Act of 1964 prohibits discrimination against employees on the basis of race, color, religion, sex, or national origin. One section of the act, 42 U.S.C,. 2000e(j), gives strong protection to religious workers:

> The term "religion" includes all aspects of religious observance and practice, as well as belief, unless an

employer demonstrates that he is unable to reasonably accommodate to an employee's or prospective employee's religious observance or practice without undue hardship on the conduct of the employer's business.

In other words, if you refuse on bona fide religious grounds to attend a New Age-oriented business seminar, your employer may not fire you, or demote you, or refuse to promote you, or discriminate against you in any way, unless he can demonstrate that attendance at that seminar is so essential to his business that excusing you from the seminar would cause his business undue hardship. This would be pretty difficult for an employer to demonstrate.

I am not saying all or even most business seminars contain New Age concepts, or that you should refuse to attend any seminar that might teach something you disagree with. I do urge you to be on the lookout for New Age concepts in many of these seminars, however. And if you decide, based upon your religious convictions, that you should not attend, the Civil Rights Act of 1964 may protect you in doing so.

(10) Legislate against Satanic practices.

In 1989 a group of Pennsylvania legislators prepared a bill to adopt a new law called the "Satanic Rituals and Practices Prohibition Act." The bill contained several whereas clauses, including:

WHEREAS the organized, ritualistic, social glorification of Satan promotes an outlook dominated by the principle of evil, and the proliferation of evil practices that flow as a consequences of that evil outlook.

WHEREAS the proliferation of evil practices constitutes a threat to the inherent rights of mankind stipulated in Article I, Section 1 of the Pennsylvania Constitution.

WHEREAS the Framers of the Pennsylvania Constitution, who state in the Preamble, "We the people ... grateful to Almighty God for the blessings of civil and religious liberty and humbly invoking His guidance ... " did not intend to promote evil (Satanic) practices in the Commonwealth of Pennsylvania.

WHEREAS satanic rituals "tend to corrupt" the individuals participating in the rituals.

WHEREAS it has been well-established by professional studies that participation in the acts of mutilation, dismemberment, torture, and/or ritualistic sacrifice of animals and/or human surrogates induces a homicidal outlook in the mind of the person who participates in such acts.

"WHEREAS the U.S. Supreme Court states in *Cantwell* vs. *Connecticut* 310 U.S. 296 that one may have any religious belief one desires but one's conduct remains subject to regulations for the protection of society.

WHEREAS the U.S. Supreme Court in *Reynolds* vs. *U.S.* 98 U.S. 445 states that Congress was deprived of all legislative power over mere opinion, but was left free to reach actions which were in "violation of social duties or subversive of good order."

The General Assembly of the Commonwealth of Pennsylvania hereby enacts as follows:

This act shall be known and may be cited as the Satanic Rituals and Practices Prohibition Act.

It is the purpose of this act to protect the health and safety of the people of Pennsylvania from the menace of the organized, ritualistic social glorification of Satan

shall be prohibited. All individuals engaged in the
organized, ritualistic, social glorification of Satan shall
be deemed to be in violation of this act.

Satanic acts, practices, and rituals which constitute
the organized, ritualistic, social glorification of Satan
include, but are not strictly delimited to:

a) The consumption of human blood;

b) The ritualistic consumption of animal blood and/
or animal blood intermixed with urine and/or feces;

c) Ritualistic animal mutilations dismemberments,
and sacrifices;

d) Ritualistic use and abuse of human fetuses;

e) Ritualistic hanging, torturing, and/or crucifying
animals on crosses;

f) Ritualistic hanging, torturing, and/or crucifying
animals on inverted crosses;

g) Ritualistic sexual abuse of children, as well as
ritualistic symbolic sexual abuse of children;

h) Ritualistic sexual abuse of men and women, as
well as ritualistic symbolic sexual abuse of men and
women;

i) Ritualistic psychological abuse of children;

j) Ritualistic cannibalism.

The bill then provides for escalating fines and
imprisonment for first, second, and third offend-
ers.

Although it is doubtful that the Founding Fathers intended the First Amendment to protect
Satanism, it is quite possible that the Supreme
Court would rule that the First Amendment does
give a person the right to worship Satan. In this
and many other areas of constitutional law, the
Supreme Court has strayed far from the intent of
the Framers. But it is almost certain that the

Supreme Court would rule that the state has a compelling interest in preventing most if not all of the practices described above. While this bill could be improved, you might work for similar legislation in your state.

(11) Become an apologist for the Christian faith.

Today the word "apologetics" has an almost pathetic ring. We think of someone saying wimpishly, "I'm sorry, but I just happen to be a Christian. I do so hope no one is offended by that."

That's not the original meaning of the word. Originally it meant "to speak in defense." An apologetic is a forthright, forceful defense of the Christian faith. Jude exhorts us to "earnestly contend for the faith which was once delivered unto the saints" (Jude 3), and Peter tells us to "be ready always to give an answer to every man that asketh you a reason of the hope that is in you with meekness and fear" (1 Pet. 3:15).

I suggest that one reason for the popularity of the New Age movement today is the failure of religious liberalism to satisfy the inner needs of men.

By failing to present a clear gospel and a clear divine standard, by failing to stand for the absolute truths of Scripture, and by frequently failing to present anything more than sterile humanism with a thin Christian veneer, the religious liberalism of many mainline denominations has left many people groping in the dark as they search for transcendent meaning in life. To such people the promises of the New Age seem very tempting indeed.

Against the onslaught of the New Age movement, Christians need to clearly understand and forcefully defend the Christian faith.

(12) Be confident of God's ultimate victory.

Christian theologians differ on the interpretation of the Book of Revelation.[5] But whether premillennial, postmillennial, amillennial, panmillennial, or promillennial, all agree that Revelation comes to one conclusion: Jesus wins, and we win with Him and through Him!

This doesn't mean we're going to win every battle. The school board might deny our request. The judge may rule against us. By the time we pass from this life, the New Age movement may be even more entrenched than it is today.

But Jesus is the ultimate winner, and we will share in His victory. When you are bogged down in despair and defeat, read Revelation 19!

And while we wait for His return, we are to defend His Word faithfully, whether in victory or defeat. As Christ said to the angel of the church at Sardis, "Be watchful, and strengthen the things that remain, that are ready to die" (Rev. 3:2). God has not called us necessarily to be successful. He has called us to be faithful. He will provide the ultimate victory in a way that exceeds our fondest expectations.

And we can join Luther in that last stanza of his triumphal hymn,

> That word above all earthly powers,
> No thanks to them, abideth;
> The Spirit and the gifts are ours
> Through him who with us sideth:
> Let goods and kindred go,
> This mortal life also;
> The body they may kill:
> God's truth abideth still,
>      His kingdom is forever.

## ENDNOTES

1. C.S. Lewis, *The Screwtape Letters* (New York: MacMillan, 1961, 1968), p. 3.

2. John Dumphy, *The Humanist*, January/February 1983, p. 26.

3. See, for example, Lauren Stratford, *Satan's Underground* (Eugene, Oregon: Harvest House, 1988; Rebecca Brown, M.D., *He Came To Set the Captives Free* (Chino, California: Chick Publications, 1986); *Prepare For War* (Chino: Chick, 1987). The Satanic activities described in these books may seem incredible, but similar events are being confirmed across the nation.

4. "Touchstone: Witch's Love Letter" (February 1974), p. 9; quoted by Margot Adler, *Drawing Down the Moon* (Boston: Beacon, 1979, 1986), p. 128.

5. I regret that disagreement over eschatology is creating major conflicts among Christians today. For the record, however, I hold the premillennial, pretribulation rapture position.